Revelation 16:5

Beza's Expansion of the Rare Nomen Sacrum Form of Jehovah and I AM in the Final Triadic Declaration

NICK SAYERS

Disclaimer

The author of this work has quoted the writers of many articles and books. This does not mean that the author endorses or recommends the works of others. If the author quotes someone, it does not mean that he agrees with all of the author's tenets, statements, concepts, or words, whether in the work quoted or any other work of the author. There has been no attempt to alter the meaning of the quotes; and therefore, some of the quotes are long in order to give the entire sense of the passage.

Address All Inquiries To:
THE OLD PATHS PUBLICATIONS, INC.
142 Gold Flume Way
Cleveland, Georgia, 30528
U.S.A.

Web: www.theoldpathspublications.com
E-mail: TOP@theoldpathspublications.com

DEDICATION

This book is dedicated to every genuine Christian who has been sidetracked by the pseudo scholarship of modern text critics.

He that is first in his own cause seemeth just; but his neighbour cometh and searcheth him. - Proverbs 18:17

The first trace of "esomenos" in Beza's readings is in Beza's own handwritten notes on his 1565 edition on page 647 in preparation for the third edition of 1582.[1]

---

[1] http://doc.rero.ch/record/18245?ln=fr

ACKNOWLEDGEMENTS

This study on Revelation 16:5 has grown from the collection of information put into my website Textus-Receptus.com[2] which is constantly being updated with material defending the Textus Receptus and the King James Version. My thanks go to the following people[3]:

The author of the article on the KJV Today website[4] who has stimulated many thoughts and collected a large concise body of evidence on this and many related issues; Will Kinney[5] for his tireless efforts in defending such verses and also collecting an innumerable amount of material on this and many other subjects; also Scott Jones for his brilliant article on Jehovah[6], which while only brief, is filled with an abundance of confirmation for the Sacred Name of Jehovah. My appreciation also goes to Jeffrey Khoo[7], Thomas Holland[8], D. A. Waite[9], and Jack Moorman[10], all of whose former work on Revelation 16:5 and other such issues, has provided a platform from which I can work. The online writings of Steven Avery[11], Jeff Riddle[12], and Steve Rafalsky[13], have also

---

[2] http://textus-receptus.com/wiki/Revelation_16:5

[3] As mentioned already in the disclaimer, this does not mean I endorse anyone I quote from or from whom I have attained information. I am merely presenting an honest acknowledgment that these people produced material that lead me in a certain train of thinking which has led to the document you see today. I am certain that every one of the above mentioned people and I could debate on many other issues.

[4] https://sites.google.com/site/kjvtoday/home/translation-issues/shalt-be-or-holy-one-in-revelation-165

[5] http://brandplucked.webs.com/rev165shaltbe5810us.htm

[6] https://web.archive.org/web/20120905150114/http://www.lamblion.net/eBooks/Scott%20PDF/jehovah.pdf

[7] http://www.febc.edu.sg/BBVol15_2c.htm

[8] http://www.wilderness-cry.net/bible_study/courses/mssevidence/lesson10.html

[9] http://greatbiblehoax.blogspot.com/2011/02/d-waite-on-moorman-white-debate.html

[10] http://faithsaves.net/majority-text-moorman

[11] https://kjvonlydebate.com/2009/08/27/testing-the-textus-receptus-rev-165

been very insightful and helpful in many forums/debate groups. This private study has grown into the document you see now and has gleanings from each of the above people and others. Thanks also to Joseph Armstrong[14], David Daniels[15], and Keith Mason[16]. Special thanks to Dr. H. D. Williams[17] for the opportunity to print this information in the current book format.

It has been said, tongue in cheek, that if you copy from one source it is plagiarism, but if you copy from many sources it is "good scholarship". In this document I have copied and used the writings of the above people so frequently that it is hard for me to reference exactly where I sourced certain information from and also to distinguish which quotations are originally mine. On the TR (*www.textus-receptus.com*) website, I am constantly adding material from many different people who provide a defense for the TR/KJV position, directly from forums, websites, debate groups, YouTube clips, or their comments on videos, and am guilty of using quotes and phrases without reference. So if you find me quoting you here or on my site, my apologies for my lack of reference, my first pursuit here has been to defend the TR/KJV reading and not provide a perfectly referenced academic treatise. This book was also written to inform those who know little about the topics involved and the entire concept could have been described in less than ten pages, but so as to not confuse those who are new to the issue, or have been duped by the pseudo-

---

[12] http://www.jeffriddle.net/2015/08/text-note-on-revelation-1117-and.html
[13] http://www.puritanboard.com/showthread.php/55296-Rev-16-5-in-the-KJV
[14] https://www.youtube.com/channel/UCXP4MCWOWaWsKonkAMx2gEg/video
[15] https://www.youtube.com/user/pdflm/videos
[16] http://www.textusreceptusbibles.com
[17] http://www.theoldpathspublications.com/

scholarship of people like White, I have provided as much material as possible in the short amount of time I have had to write this. I hope this is not an annoyance to those familiar with these issues. Some of the Latin in this article needs refinement, and any fluent volunteers are welcome to translate –

textusreceptusbibles@gmail.com

- Nick Sayers

TABLE OF CONTENTS

GENERAL INTRODUCTION

"Imagine we came across an early manuscript copy of the Constitution of the United States, and the preamble said, "We the people of the United States, in order to form a more perfect onion ..." If we were to see that line, we would know that "union" was the original word, not "onion"."-Dan Wallace[18]

This book was written in response to the false claims that the Revelation 16:5 reading of "shalt be" in the King James Version is an erroneous reading and should be considered a general defense for those who hold to either King James Only,[19] Textus Receptus Only,[20] or Ecclesiastical Text[21] positions. The issue can be clearly seen by comparing the KJV and NASB:

---

[18] Is the Original New Testament Lost? Ehrman vs Wallace (Debate Transcript) http://www.credocourses.com/blog/2016/original-new-testament-lost-ehrman-vs-wallace-debate-transcript/ Disclaimer ~ Although I disagree with Wallace on many levels concerning his method of textual criticism, I think this quotation and its implications are very pertinent to this subject.

[19] King James Only, not a self-inspired document as a small fringe element proclaim but "only" as in the best in English, which is basically the same position as Textus Receptus Only; same coin, different side; one Greek, one English. If the KJV translators had produced their own parallel Greek TR text, as Westcott and Hort did, there would be no issue on this, but they didn't. They made an English bible; they say in the preface that they checked *all* available versions. If it was in Greek, there would be no hesitation to accept it as authoritative, but they completed it in English instead. Edward F. Hills said, *"the King James Version ought to be regarded not merely as a translation of the Textus Receptus but also as an independent variety of the Textus Receptus."* (Edward F. Hills, *The King James Version Defended*, 4th edition, pp. 220, 223). There are only about 20 translatable differences between Beza's 1598 and the KJV itself. Scrivener attempted to recreate the unpublished Greek underlying the KJV in 1881. Where he falls short, the KJV is to be upheld.

[20] Textus Receptus Only, is many times the same position as KJVO, except KJVO has been associated with spurious characters and people of poor character. Some TRO people usually side with much KJVO argumentation, but reject the KJVO label as it carries baggage. The KJV is the accumulation of the many Greek editions in the reformation period. Some TRO may reject the perfection of the KJV, and may reject Beza, and favor any one of the TR editions from the 1514 Complutensian to the 1881 of Scrivener. Many times the TRO position will erroneously reject English readings like Easter, Church, and other English words, but still follow the 'basic' Greek TR.

[21] The Ecclesiastical Text position can involve people who may have either KJVO or TRO positions, but usually acquire this position due to the doctrine of preservation as

11

Revelation 16:5	
KJV	**NASB**
And I heard the angel of the waters say, Thou art righteous, O Lord, which art, and wast, **and shalt be**, because thou hast judged thus.[22]	And I heard the angel of the waters saying, "Righteous are You, who are and who were, **O Holy One**, because You judged these things;[23]

In this book, it will be revealed that Theodore Beza's reading that underlies the KJV is undeniably correct, and that the scholarship of many of his detractors is flawed. It should be noted that this book has been principally written in response to James White's erroneous position, and the format has been designed around refuting the false claims and accusations he has made on his popular *Dividing Line* program on YouTube. But I have also kept in mind that this book needed to provide material and information to generally educate the church concerning this verse with elements that were rudimentary to Beza and the King James Version translators in their scholarly generation, but today may be obscured by the cloud of skeptical textual criticism.

James White[24], who is the director of *Alpha and Omega Ministries*, has made claims that the reading of "and shalt be" in Revelation 16:5 is "an irrefutable error in the KJV"[25] and that the 1611 translators slavishly followed Theodore Beza's 1598 edition of the Textus Receptus in which this so called error originates. White

---

outlined in the Westminster Confession of Faith or 2nd London Baptist Confession. It has the belief that the church carries the true words of God, not heretics, unsaved Scholars, or the world. The true Church will recognize the true Scriptures and use them. Theodore Letis and Edward F. Hills are part of this group. It can be called Confessional Bibliology or slanderously (by James White) Textual Traditionalism.

[22] http://textus-receptus.com/wiki/Revelation_16:5

[23] New American Standard Bible (NASB) Copyright © 1960, 1962, 1963, 1968, 1971, 1972, 1973, 1975, 1977, 1995 by The Lockman Foundation.

[24] http://www.aomin.org/aoblog/index.php/about/

[25] White, James. The King James Only Controversy: Can You Trust the Modern Translations? (Updated June 1, 2009 Expanded edition), Minneapolis: Bethany House Publishers; Updated, Paperback: 368 pages, p. 237, ISBN-13: 978-0764206054

considers the reading of "shalt be" as a trump card against those who defend the King James Version or Textus Receptus on this point, who, he claims, would usually point to a majority text reading to defend their position, but seem to have the tables turned concerning this verse with the KJV reading being considered as a minority reading, or specifically here, a conjecture with zero evidence. White's claims about this verse in his book *The King James Only Controversy*[26], in his *YouTube* videos[27], as well as in debates such as the Jack Moorman debate of 2011[28] are unscholarly and mostly false, as will be revealed in this book.

In August 2016 I discovered that the 1549 Ethiopic version has the same "shalt be" reading in Revelation 16:5 as Beza's TR and the KJV. I created a blogspot[29] concerning this which was discovered by White the following day, who proceeded to rebuke me on his *Dividing Line*[30] program after I presented the Ethiopic evidence for the KJV reading. He warned people to stay away from my teaching.[31] To get a perception of White's position on the issue and his usual response to those who defend Revelation 16:5, in this 2002 transcript of the 1995 Ankerberg show he said:

> "But to Dr. Strouse, what about places where those King James translators followed conjectural emendations? Theodore Beza, for example, in Revelation 16:5 looked at the Greek text and all the Greek texts say the same thing, but he didn't like the way it went. And so he changed the word "holy" to the future form of the verb "to be," sort of, to make it nice and poetic and rhythmic. And

---

[26] White, James (1995), The King James Only Controversy: Can You Trust the Modern Translations?, Minneapolis: Bethany House, p. 248, ISBN 1-55661-575-2,

[27] https://www.youtube.com/user/AominOrg/videos

[28] https://www.youtube.com/watch?v=PHR8wJAjNFo

[29] http://textusreceptusbibles.blogspot.com.au/2016/09/beza-vindicated_1.html

[30] https://www.youtube.com/watch?v=Uqh4Jc2VkAM (from about the 25-minute mark)

[31] See Appendix 1 at end of this book for the full transcript.

your King James this day reads that way, even though there's not a question about it on anyone's part as to what that passage actually reads. Why should I take Theodore Beza's conjectural emendation where he decides a reading on the basis of what he likes and say that the mass of Christians believe this when nobody before Theodore Beza ever had the idea that Revelation 16:5 read that way? Why should I believe that?"[32]

White also says in his book *The King James Only Controversy*:

Every Greek text – not just Alexandrian texts, but all Greek texts, Majority Text, the Byzantine text, every manuscript, the entire manuscript tradition – reads "O Holy One," containing the Greek phrase ὁ ὅσιος ("ho hosios.") So why does the KJV read "and shalt be"? Because John Calvin's successor at Geneva, Theodore Beza, conjectured that the original read differently. To use his word, "ex vetusto bonae fidei manuscripto codice restitui." Beza believed there was sufficient similarity between the Greek terms ὅσιος and ἐσόμενος (the future form, "shall be") to allow him to make the change to harmonize the text with other such language in Revelation. *But he had no manuscript evidence in support of his conjecture.*

For the KJV Only advocate, there is simply no way out of this problem. Those who appeal to the Byzantine text-type are refuted, for it reads ὁ ὅσιος. Those who appeal to the Majority Text founder on the same reality....[33] (emphasis original)

[32] The King James Controversy Revisited - 2002
https://www.jashow.org/articles/general/the-king-james-controversy-revisited-program-3/
on the Ankerberg show, with Dr. Kenneth Barker, Dr. Don Wilkins, Dr. Daniel B. Wallace, Dr. James White, Dr. Samuel Gipp, Dr. Thomas Strouse, Dr. Joseph Chambers.)
[33] White, James (1995), The King James Only Controversy: Can You Trust the Modern Translations?, Minneapolis: Bethany House, p. 248, ISBN 1-55661-575-2,

White then shows some pictures in his book of Erasmus' edition, Coverdale, and Geneva, which do not have the KJV reading "shalt be", but say "and holy"; he then concludes:

> As one can see, the King James Version reading at Revelation 16:5 arose from Theodore Beza's conjectural emendation *and was unknown to history prior to that time.* (emphasis original)[34]

White places a footnote here which basically says that even if those in the future prove him wrong on this issue, they are being desperate and rejecting the very words of Beza who said he merely conjectured on this issue:

> "Lest in desperation a King James Only advocate make the attempt, Tischendorf's notes on the term only confirm my assertion. He notes that "cop aeth" omit ὁ ὅσιος, but the KJV reading is not to be found even here, as ἐσόμενος is not put in its place. Instead Tischendorf's notes indicate Beza as the reading's source. Further, Tregelles' text, though indicating some translations omitted ὁ ὅσιος again indicates that the KJV reading is nowhere in the Greek manuscript tradition. Likewise, Hoskier's massive work on the text of the Apocalypse nowhere indicates the appearance of Beza's conjecture. *Quite simply, before Beza, no Christian had ever read the text the way the KJV has it today.*" (italics added) [35]

This book will provide a framework wherein the bible believer can observe the biblical and historical case for the inclusion of "shalt be" and will also reveal that *all* evidence points to Beza's reading, and only those

---

[34] White, James. The King James Only Controversy: Can You Trust the Modern Translations? (Updated June 1, 2009 Expanded edition), Minneapolis: Bethany House Publishers; Updated, Paperback: 368 pages, p. 240, ISBN-13: 978-0764206054
[35] Ibid. p. 240-241, footnote.

willingly ignorant will choose to follow the inferior reading of "holy" after examining the facts presented below. I will also reveal how James White does not understand the basics of what Beza said in his footnotes, and looking at his debates, videos, and book concerning this subject, only exposes his illiteracy, leaving him much like the king with no clothes. Proud scholars like White place doubt upon 254 passages in the TR/KJV. He is an enemy of the traditional scriptures.

Theodore Beza was a world class biblical scholar, an expert in several languages, and one who associated with those considered the upper echelon of biblical scholarship, who provided material that fueled the reformation in many languages. Because Beza had provided such a massive amount of biblical data, from heading up the English Geneva Bible, Geneva French, many Greek and Latin editions, commentaries, dictionaries, and so much literature on the Greek and Hebrew biblical text for so many years, I would suggest that Beza's familiarity with the text and with similar textual issues, revealed to him that the established reading of "holy" was clearly an error. For one to reject the obvious conclusion of "shalt be", one should firstly show that they are on the same level of scholarship as Beza or the KJV translators on this issue to provide an adequate refutation, or at least understand Beza's footnotes properly. White, who was one of the critical consultants for the New American Standard Bible,[36] doesn't have the goods to even understand the basics of this issue, but simply slanders and misquotes people, in order to win his debate points. In this article I will show to the reader that the manuscript evidence does indeed point to *esomenos*, and that once the foundation is laid, one will not be able to read the text again without

---

[36] http://www.lockman.org/nasb/nasbprin.php

seeing this reading as correct, no matter which manuscript you read.

Beza reconstructed the original reading of what became a corrupted, contaminated, nonsensical, and illegible textual reading, but it was originally altered to read "holy" in the early church for a specific purpose, and after reading this book, you will be fully aware of the reasons Beza saw this corruption, and his remedy for it. A cursory look just at the English translations preceding the KJV shows the confusion surrounding this verse as we shall see. God is not the Author of confusion. Beza's restitution of (L.) eris / (G.) ἐσόμενος is far from being just an educated guess as some have claimed. An experienced and proficient scholar with a broad knowledge of the writer of the text, Greek and Hebrew languages, and style of the time, knows error when he sees it. This is called intrinsic probabilities.[37]

It must also be noted that when White rebuked me on his *Dividing Line* program for sharing with the world that the 1549 Ethiopic bible has the same TR reading as Beza, he also issued a challenge to myself and all KJVO/TRO people to read the evidence concerning Revelation 16:5 in his book and come to conclusions. That is the reason for this book. I expected White to be vitriolic and mocking at the finding, as I have previously encountered such behavior from White in his forum

---

[37] Agnostic/Atheist text critic Bart Ehrman in *Whose Word is It?*, correctly defined intrinsic probabilities when he said:

"...*intrinsic* probabilities — probabilities based on what the author of the text was himself most likely to have written. We are able to study, of course, the writing style, the vocabulary, and the theology of an author. When two or more variant readings are preserved among our manuscripts, and one of them uses words or stylistic features otherwise not found in that author's work, or if it represents a point of view that is at variance with what the author otherwise embraces, then it is unlikely that that is what the author wrote — especially if another attested reading coincides perfectly well with the author's writing elsewhere." 131 Ehrman, Bart. Whose Word is It?: The Story Behind Who Changed The New Testament and Why. (1 Mar 2006) A&C Black, 256 pages, p. 131. ISBN:0-8264-9129-4

about 10 years before, when, I politely asked him if I could present a view about Easter that he may not have seen before. He said it was fine for me to present my case. After I began to post a few sentences concerning the etymology of Easter[38], White asked me some accusatory questions about my understanding of the word "anachronism" as did others in the chat group. As I was attempting to answer them, and before I could even state my position, White became very annoyed and irrational and then slanderously called me a Ruckmanite and permanently banned me from his forum. So to see White mock those who translate the Textus Receptus / Reformation Text, and to mock at the evidence revealing that the "shalt be" reading is indeed in bibles older than Beza's, was not a shock, but a predictable reaction. In stark contrast concerning Easter, world leading expert on the English language David Crystal[39] read the first article and said it was a good article and that the information was correct and gave me some pointers on it. This alone shows you the difference between a genuine scholar and a pseudo scholar. For those interested in what White originally said about the Ethiopic evidence on his program see Appendix 1.

So this book is not really written with a great expectation of changing White's mind, which seems to be already made up no matter what evidence is presented, but it is for those who are being influenced by him, who are more humble, and looking for genuine answers. It is also written for those who accept the reading but need ammo against the claims of White.

---

[38] http://www.easterau.com ~ I wrote "Our word Easter is of Saxon origin and of precisely the same import with its German cognate Ostern. The latter is derived from the old Teutonic form of auferstehen / auferstehung, that is - resurrection." - Eusebius' Ecclesiastical History, Translated by C. F. Cruse, Hendrickson Publishers, p 437
[39] https://en.wikipedia.org/wiki/David_Crystal

CHAPTER 1

That men may know that thou, whose name alone is
JEHOVAH, art the most high over all the earth. - Psalm 83:18

1.1 THE TETRAGRAMMATON

The Tetragrammaton as it appears in the 1611 King James Version

Firstly, the key to understanding the issue surrounding
Revelation 16:5 involves a basic understanding of the
Tetragrammaton and its importance. The word
tetragrammaton (Gr. Τετραγράμματον) is transliterated
for us English speakers from the Greek which simply

means "*four letters*", and is the Hebrew theonym[40] יְהֹוָה Yehovah, which is commonly transliterated into Latin letters as YHWH and erroneously pronounced Yahweh by some as we shall see soon. It is the most significant name of God used in the Hebrew Bible. The name is derived from a verb that means "to be", "to exist", "to cause to become", or "to come to pass". It appears in every book of the Old Testament, with the exception of Esther, Ecclesiastes, and Song of Solomon.

Jehovah is an anglicized pronunciation of the Hebrew tetragrammaton יְהֹוָה Yehovah and appears 6,518 times in the traditional Masoretic Text, in addition to 305 instances of יֱהֹוִה Jehovee.

Primarily, it must be noted that the etymology of יְהֹוָה Jehovah comes from הָוָה hava.[41] Historically, some have claimed that Jehovah comes from 1943[42] which is הֹוָה hovah - a ruin, disaster – but this is false. The etymological link is clearly to הָוָה hava - 1933 and הֹוָה hovah is simply homophonic. You can clearly see the distinction here from a basic search on blueletterbible.org:

הֹוָה Lexical number H1943	הָוָה Lexical number H1933
Transliteration = hovah	Transliteration = hava'
Meaning = Misfortune, calamity, adversity.[42]	Meaning = Shall be, may be, will occur.[41]

יְהֹוָה Jehovah is numbered in any modern concordance as H3068. The definition of Jehovah lists the root word as H1961 hayah, "to become", which comes from the primitive root H1933 hava, "shall be".

---

[40] http://textus-receptus.com/wiki/Theonym - A theonym is a proper name of a deity. The study of theonyms is a branch of onomastics, the study of the origin, history, and use of proper names.
[41] ...h1933
[42] ...h1943

יְהֹוָה Lexical number H3068	הָיָה Lexical number H1961
Transliteration = Yehovah	Transliteration = hayah
Meaning = Jehovah, name of the supreme God of the Hebrews.[43]	Meaning = To be, to become, exist.[44]

Jehovah clearly comes from *hava* which means "shall be". Take careful notice with this etymological link. This word in Greek would directly translate as ἐσόμενος (esomenos), which is *exactly* what Theodore Beza placed in Revelation 16:5 and which translates as "shalt be" in English. This is because the word Jehovah means the Existing One, *"who is, and was, and shalt be"*. The Jehovah/hava link is elementary to Hebraists. For example, the 1814 Elements of Hebrew Grammar below shows us that the name *Jehovah* stems from *hava*:

Examples of י prefixed and postfixed.

י prefixed, commonly forms proper names.

עקב To supplant.   יעקב Jacob.
חנן To show favour.   יוחנן Joannes, Grati-
                                        osus.
צחק To laugh.   יצחק Isaac.
הוה To be, to exist.   יהוה *Jehovah.*

Sometimes common nouns are formed in the same manner.

1814 Elements of Hebrew Grammar reveals that Jehovah comes from hava. James White said this is untrue on Twitter.

---

[43] ...h3068
[44] ...h1961

The example above is revealing that at times, the Yod - י is prefixed to proper names, such as to הָוָה hava to form Jehovah (Je - hovah). Notice *hava* clearly means "to be, to exist". This shows us that *hava* has a direct link to "ἐσόμενος ", "shalt be". *To be* or not *to be*? That is the question White cannot seem to answer with any factual evidence:

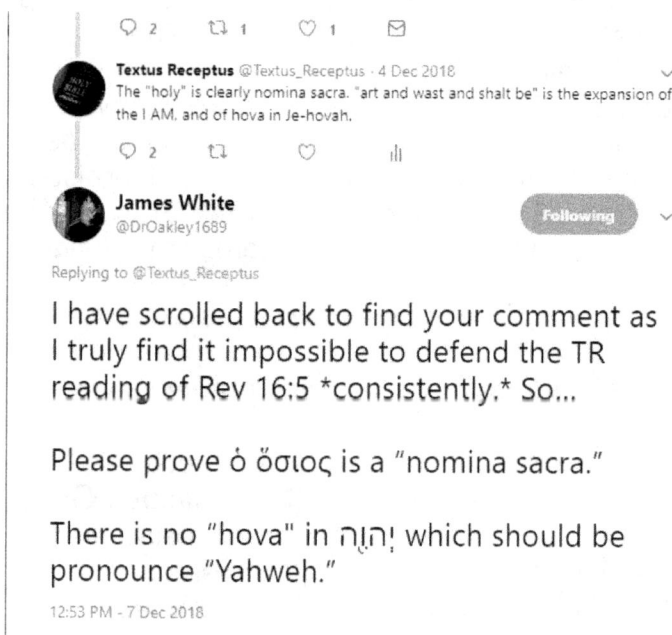

Textus Receptus @Textus_Receptus · 4 Dec 2018
The "holy" is clearly nomina sacra. "art and wast and shalt be" is the expansion of the I AM. and of hova in Je-hovah.

James White
@DrOakley1689

Following

Replying to @Textus_Receptus

I have scrolled back to find your comment as I truly find it impossible to defend the TR reading of Rev 16:5 *consistently.* So...

Please prove ὁ ὅσιος is a "nomina sacra."

There is no "hova" in יְהֹוֶה which should be pronounce "Yahweh."

12:53 PM - 7 Dec 2018

In an exchange on Twitter in late 2018, White demonstrates his ignorance of the *hava* link, having a presupposition that *Yahweh* is the phonetical rendering of the Tetragrammaton, he rejects the logical conclusion of Hebraists.[45]

---

[45] White initially said he would not read my book (original 2016 draft), so I approached him on Twitter and posted some of the info in this book. Since then he has called me a cultist, said I think like a Mormon, and I am just like a Jehovah's Witness in my mentality. He refused to deal with my book/article, but merely quoted my small tweets and did an entire program on them, without once going to my freely available info about this.

1.2 The Name Jehovah

Many modern Hebrews will not even pronounce the Tetragrammaton literally. If you listen to an audio of the Hebrew bible, you will hear that the speaker, most times, will pronounce the term *Adonai* where *Jehovah* is written, but this has not always been the case, and the following evidence shows that the name was well known in Israel and pronounced frequently in the Old and New Testament periods.

Scott Jones wrote an excellent article in 2001 that clarified this concept. In his article he shows how, by examining the names of several Israelites, we learn that the Sacred Name Jehovah was frequently used in Israel, and also that issues concerning the Sacred Name have roots even in the biblical record itself. Scott Jones' chart shows how the "eh" sound, unique to Jehovah (and not in Yahweh), was modified so that people did not mention the Sacred Name by accident. Jones states:

> Ginsburg then goes on to demonstrate from the text and the Masorah that the following names were shortened so as not to accidentally pronounce the Tetragrammaton at the wrong time, or in the wrong place, or by the wrong person.[46]

Jones placed the following chart in his article, revealing this concept of removing the "eh" sound out of names. JEHO and JO are compared:

---

[46]https://web.archive.org/web/20120905150114/http://www.lamblion.net/eBooks/Scott%20PDF/jehovah.pdf

JEHOachaz	יְהוֹאָחָז	JOachaz	יוֹאָחָז
JEHOash	יְהוֹאָשׁ	JOash	יוֹאָשׁ
JEHOzabad	יְהוֹזָבָד	JOzabad	יוֹזָבָד
JEHOhanan	יְהוֹחָנָן	JOhanan	יוֹחָנָן
JEHOiada	יְהוֹיָדָע	JOiada	יוֹיָדָע
JEHOiachin	יְהוֹיָכִין	JOiachin	יוֹיָכִין
JEHOiakim	יְהוֹיָקִים	JOiakim	יוֹיָקִים
JEHOiarib	יְהוֹיָרִיב	JOiarib	יוֹיָרִיב
JEHOnadab	יְהוֹנָדָב	JOnadab	יוֹנָדָב
JEHOnathan	יְהוֹנָתָן	JOnathan	יוֹנָתָן
JEHOseph	יְהוֹסֵף	JOseph	יוֹסֵף
JEHOzadak	יְהוֹצָדָק	JOzadak	יוֹצָדָק
JEHOram	יְהוֹרָם	JOram	יוֹרָם
JEHOshaphat	יְהוֹשָׁפָט	JOshaphat	יוֹשָׁפָט

Jones stated:

> Thus, it is clear how the ancient Jews viewed the correct pronunciation of the Tetragrammaton, for without exception the first two syllables in the above names are identical in pronunciation to the traditional pronunciation of the Tetragrammaton. Further, the above names, as Ginsburg notes, are all derivatives of the Tetragrammaton. Like father, like son. The first two syllables in these names was pronounced the same way the Tetragrammaton was pronounced, which is why the Jews took safeguards to shorten these names in the first place. If the Jewish guardians of the Hebrew Scriptures did not consider Jehovah to be the correct pronunciation of the Ineffable Name, the above exercise in shortening the names would have been superfluous.

Jones then quoted the Noted Hebraist Davidson, On The Tetragrammaton Davidson in The Analytical Hebrew and Chaldee Lexicon, Hendrickson Publishers, page 171, where he says as follows:

יְהֹוָה the most sacred name of God, expressive of His *eternal, Self-existence*, first communicated to the Hebrews, Ex. 3:14, comp. chap. 6:3. This name appears to be composed of יְהֹו (fut. of הָוָה, like יְהִי from הָיָה) and וְה (preterite by aphaeresis for הָוָה), the verb *to be* being twice repeated as in Ex. 3:14. If we supply אֲשֶׁר between these words we obtain nearly the same sense as expressed there in the words אֶהְיֶה אֲשֶׁר אֶהְיֶה . The Jews who (from an early date) believed this name incommunicable, substituted, in the pronunciation, the consonants of אֲדֹנָי , the vowels being alike in both words (with the exception of simple and composite Sheva), and according to these the punctuators suited the vowels of the prefixes when coming to stand before יְהֹוָה , as מֵיהוֹם , לַיהוָה , בַּאדֹנָי according to מֵאֲדֹנָי , לַאדֹנָי , בַּאדֹנָי . Where, however, יְהֹוָה is already preceded by אֲדֹנָי , to avoid repetition, they furnished it with the vowels of אֱלֹהִים , in order that it be pronounced with its consonants, so that אֲדֹנָי יְהֹוָה is to be read אֲדֹנָי אֱלֹהִים . The punctuators seem to intimate the originality of the vowels of יְהֹוָה by not pointing Yod with Hhateph Pattah (יֲהֹוָה) to indicate the reading of אֲדֹנָי just as they point it with Hhateph-Segol to indicate the reading of אֱלֹהִים . We could, moreover, not account for the abbreviated forms יְהוֹ , יוֹ prefixed to so many proper names, unless we consider the vowels of יְהֹוָה original.

Note the conclusion of Davidson:

We could, moreover, not account for the abbreviated forms יְהוֹ, יוֹ prefixed to so many proper names, *unless we consider the vowels of יְהֹוָה original.*[47]

When I was in the Philippines at a bible conference in 2004, a pastor I was preaching for was named Pastor Jesse. He actually had to change his name because his real name is Pastor "Jesus", which would make for some interesting misunderstandings during worship times. Anyone familiar with Mexico or the Philippines knows that there are many men named "Jesus" (*hay sooce*) there. For future generations, this in itself is enough proof to demonstrate that a Christian or Catholic influence had been on the nation. Likewise, it is also

---

[47] The Analytical Hebrew & Chaldee Lexicon, 1848, by Benjamin Davidson ISBN 0913573035

very basic logic that because so many people in the bible were named after Jehovah, obviously the name was frequently known and used by the common people. Imagine in 2000 years equating that while millions have been called "Jesus" in Mexico and the Philippines that no one ever mentioned his name, or that the name was actually Yahcoobooon or something like that? That would be absurd. This is why we know for certain that Jehovah was widely used and also that Jehovah/Yehovah is His name, not Yahweh. Hallelujah for the obvious. Even Benjamin Netanyahu's surname has Yahu or Yeho as in Yehovah in it. This is plain as the noonday sun if you are open to common sense. It is not Benjamin Netan-yahweh. For example, Yehonatan means "Yehovah has given" whereas Nethanyahu means "given of Yehovah".[48]

The following chart from www.seekingtruth.info reveals this concept very vividly in Hebrew writings in Hebrew manuscripts Jeho/Yeho is in each one of these names:

---

[48] http://seekingtruth.info/blog/hebrew-theophoric-names-and-the-name-of-god/

יְהוֹאָחָז Yeho'achaz　　יְחוֹעַדָּה Yeho'adah

יְחוֹאָשׁ Yehoash　　יְחוֹעָדָן Yeho'adan

יְהוֹזָבָד Yehozavad　　יְהוֹצָדָק Yehotzadak

יְהוֹחָנָן Yehochanan　　יְחוֹרָם Yehoram

יְהוֹרָדָע Yehoyada　　יְהוֹשֶׁבַע Yehosheva

יְהוֹיָכִין Yehoyakhin　　יְהוֹשַׁבְעַת Yehoshav'at

יְהוֹיָקִים Yehoyakim　　יְהוֹשֻׁעַ Yehoshua

יְהוֹנָדָב Yehonadav　　יְהוֹשָׁפָט Yehoshafat

יְהוֹנָתָן Yehonatan　　יְהוָֹה Yehovah

So how did Yeho/Jeho get into all of those Hebrew names?
Perhaps they were named after Someone? [49]

James White falsely calls God Yah'weh. Many "scholars" would have us squabling over YHVH YHWH Yahweh Yahveh Yaveh Yaweh Yahowe Yahoweh Jahaveh Jahaweh Yahaveh Yahaweh Jahuweh Yahuweh Jahuwah Yahuwah Yahuah Yah Jah Yahu Yahoo Yaohu Jahu Yahvah Jahvah Jahve Jahveh Yahve Yahwe Yauhu

---

49 http://seekingtruth.info/blog/hebrew-theophoric-names-and-the-name-of-god/

Yawhu Iahu Iahou Iahoo Iahueh. But White emphatically says it is Yah'weh. I have found that a presupposition in support of Yahweh hinders many people from correctly understanding the issues surrounding Revelation 16:5. That is why understanding that the correct name of God is Jehovah, and not Yahweh, is a very important foundation. Many already have cognitive dissidence when it comes to the name Jehovah, being in association with the cult of the Jehovah's Witnesses and also a name mocked by modern text critics.

While many claim that the name was not spoken frequently, the bible actually encouraged people to use the name in Israel in Deuteronomy 6:13,[50] 10:20,[51] and it also condemned those who did not do it in Jeremiah 10:25.[52] Superstition and a misinterpretation of two verses, Exodus 20:7[53] and Leviticus 24:16,[54] has blurred the certainty of frequent uttering. The expression in Exodus 20:7 לשוא (lassaw) correctly translated "in vain" also carries the meaning "in support of falsehood", or "lying".

So while there have been issues with the pronunciation of the Sacred Name which still linger with us today, the name represented by the tetragrammaton is most certainly Jehovah/Yehovah. Modern text critics cannot refute Jones' article. They simply turn to endless manuscript genealogies and flawed etymologies that

---

[50] Thou shalt fear the LORD thy God, and serve him, and shalt swear by his name. Deuteronomy 6:13
[51] Thou shalt fear the LORD thy God; him shalt thou serve, and to him shalt thou cleave, and swear by his name. Deuteronomy 10:20
[52] Pour out thy fury upon the heathen that know thee not, and upon the families that call not on thy name: for they have eaten up Jacob, and devoured him, and consumed him, and have made his habitation desolate. Jeremiah 10:25
[53] Thou shalt not take the name of the LORD thy God in vain; for the LORD will not hold him guiltless that taketh his name in vain. Exodus 20:7
[54] And he that blasphemeth the name of the LORD, he shall surely be put to death, and all the congregation shall certainly stone him: as well the stranger, as he that is born in the land, when he blasphemeth the name of the LORD, shall be put to death. Leviticus 24:16

never seem to come up with a definitive answer. I challenge James White, Daniel Wallace, Bart Ehrman, H. J. de Jonge, Jan Krans or any other text critic to refute Jones on this issue.

Agnostic/Atheist Bart Ehrman summarizes the basic understanding of most Textual Critics today:

"In a lot of Bibles – you may have noticed this (or you may not have) – there is a difference in the Old Testament between the word "Lord" (first letter capitalized) and the word "LORD" (all four letters capitalized). The first word translates ADONAI and the second word translates the tetragrammaton YHWH. That's how, when you're reading a translation, you can tell if the tetragrammaton is being used.

But some translators took the tetragrammaton with the vowels of Adonai and created an English word for it. In some European languages the letters Y and J are equivalents (sound the same), as are W and V (think: German). If you spell the name YHWH as JHVH and add the vowels of ADONAI, you get JEHOVAH. That's a made-up English word, not a Hebrew word (and not, before this, an English word).

People who claim that JEHOVAH is the divine name are kind of right but not really. The divine name was probably Yahweh. Technically speaking the name Jehovah doesn't occur in the Old Testament.

And it certainly does not occur in the New Testament, which was not written in Hebrew, so that it never uses the tetragrammaton.

When the Old Testament came to be translated into Greek both Yahweh and Adonai were translated by the Greek word κυριος, which in English letters is KURIOS. It is the Geek word for "Lord." It is a word that can be used to refer to your employer, your master, your superior, or to God, or ... to the personal name of God. And so when the New Testament refers to God as "Lord," it is not clear if it is calling him by his personal name or if it is designating him as the Lord. But in neither case, in my judgment, does it make sense to translate the term using the made up English word Jehovah."[55]

This is a typical concept amongst modern text critics and most would be in agreement with Ehrman here. I don't distinguish much difference between White and Ehrman or even the Jehovah's Witnesses on the issue of textual criticism. They are all on the wrong side of the fence, just at differing degrees of error. Listening to White debate Ehrman is like an Irish Catholic debating a Roman Catholic; they are birds of a feather. White simply agrees with Ehrman most of the time concerning which verses need to be deleted from the Textus Receptus.

Upon examination with the biblical record, provided by Scott Jones, we can see these modern textual critics are completely wrong when it comes to the Sacred Name of Jehovah. James White, insistently says Jehovah is a false pronunciation of the Tetragrammaton:

> "Now, "Jehovah" is a false pronunciation of the Hebrew word "YHWH," correctly pronounced "Yahweh." This is God's "personal" name in the Old Testament"[56]

White is completely wrong here. Anyone can easily recognize that the pronunciation for the tetragrammaton is clearly *Jehovah* and not *Yahweh*.

---

[55] https://www.jehovahs-witness.com/topic/156150002/bart-ehrman-answers-my-question
[56] http://vintage.aomin.org/MEMVER.html

The authors of the New Testament whose words were inspired by God translated the Hebrew Jehovah/Yehovah as the Greek *Kurios*, which means "Lord". That is why the KJV translators translated Jehovah as LORD in the Old Testament. One important feature when learning translation methodology is examining how words are carried across (translated) from the Old Testament into the New Testament by the original writers. The King James Version translators knew that if God translated the Hebrew Jehovah/Yehovah as the Greek *Kurios* without any issues, then such methods were also safe to replicate into the English tongue.

The King James has:

    Jehovah = LORD
    Jehovee = GOD
    Adonai = Lord
    Elohim = God

The Greek New Testament writers equated that Jehovah is Kurios, and the KJV translators simply follows suit in the Old Testament (except in 7 places where Jah (*yah*) is used with Jehovah/Jehovee - thus they transliterated it Jehovah in English). Jah (*yah*) is simply short for the name Jehovah as seen in the name Elijah (El - i – Jah - *Elohim is my Jehovah*) and of course in the universal word "Hallelujah" (praise Jehovah) from *hallalu*, plural imperative of *hallel* "to praise".

The name Jehovah is seen first in Genesis 2:4 as "LORD" in the King James Version. John Calvin, whom Beza succeeded in Geneva, summarized the Hebrew etymology of Jehovah in his *Commentary on Genesis*:

> ...Consequently, it is to be traced to "a Hebrew etymology." We need not follow him into the discussion

on the right pronunciation of the word, and the use of the vowel points belonging to, (Adonai); it may suffice to state, that he deduces the name (Jehovah,) from the future of the verb or, **to be**. Hence the meaning of the appellation may be expressed in the words, "He who is **to be** (for ever)." This derivation of the name Jehovah he regards as being confirmed "by all the passages of Scripture, in which a derivation of the name is either expressly given or simply hinted." And, beginning with the Book of Revelation, at the title ὁ ὢν καὶ ὁ ἦν καὶ **ὁ ερχόμενος**, "who is, and was, and **is to come**," he goes upward through the sacred volume, quoting the passages which bear upon the question, till he comes to the important passage in Exodus in. 13-16, in which God declares his name to be, **"I am that I am."** "Everything created," he adds, "remains not like itself, but is continually changing under circumstances, God only, because he is the being, is always the same; and because he is always the same, is the being."[57]

Notice that according to Calvin, Jehovah is *"from the future of the verb or, **to be**. Hence the meaning of the appellation may be expressed in the words, "He who is **to be** (for ever)."* He then goes on to link the triadic declarations in Revelation with the name of Jehovah. Ερχόμενος (is to come) is closely related to Beza's ἐσόμενος (shalt be) as we shall see later.

Dr. Bullinger gives the following definition of the word "Jehovah" in the Companion Bible saying the Triadic Declaration is from Jehovah's etymology:

---

[57] http://www.sacred-texts.com/chr/calvin/cc01/cc01007.htm

"Jehovah means the Eternal, the Immutable One, He Who Was and is and **is to come**". So when we read "I am Jehovah, that is My Name" we are reading, I am "the Eternal, the Immutable One, He Who Was and is and **is to come**", that is Who I am.

Exodus 6:3 is also helpful in establishing how "Name" is used as a figure of speech to enhance the truth of Who God is. That verse reads, "I appeared to Abraham, to Isaac and to Jacob as God Almighty, but by **My Name, Jehovah**, I did not make Myself known to them". In other words, God had appeared to Abraham, Isaac and Jacob but not as **"the Eternal, Immutable One".** but as "God Almighty". But when God appeared to Moses, He made Himself known as Who He is, His very essence, i.e. **Eternal.** [58]

1.3 The Name Yahweh

To fully understand the depth of White's error on this subject, one only has to look at the name he unwittingly utters from his lips when claiming to pronounce the most Sacred Name of our God. The spelling *Jahweh* was used in German since the 1850s. The spelling *Yahweh* in English (ensuring the pronunciation of the initial consonant as /j/) first appears in the 1860s. Many Christians have been taught by modern text critics that this is the Sacred Name of God. Dr. Thomas M. Strouse of the Dean Burgon Society has written an informative article on Yahweh[59], but let me take this information a step further. Steven Avery has a forum[60] with a plethora

---

[58] http://www.therain.org/appendixes/app4.html
[59] http://deanburgonsociety.org/CriticalTexts/yahweh.htm
[60] http://www.purebibleforum.com/forumdisplay.php?85-Jehovah-or-yahweh Disclaimer: Steven Avery has long been accused as being a modalist, although he has said that he has attended churches that are Trinitarian and Trinity lite. He says that he cannot agree with some of the creeds because they are not entirely scriptural. He has been banned from some forums due to this ambiguous position. To the best of my ability, I have

of information about this, which I recommend people use to further investigate this issue, as I am only going to brief this topic here. *Yahweh* is actually the exact ancient pronunciation of the Roman god *Jupiter*. This is the basic conclusion of even a cursory glance at the issue. So far we have learned that based upon the Hebrew Bible, there is no way that *Yahweh* is a theophoric name in Hebrew but *Jehovah* is. Let's examine the claim that *Yahweh* is *Jupiter*.

Consider these two basic points:

1) *Yahweh* in English is the vocalization equivalent to *IOVE* in classical Latin. The classical IOVE is pronounced as Yahweh = ee-ah-w-eh:

> "**i**" is pronounced "**ee**" as in the word sh**ee**p.
> "**o**" is pronounced "**ah**" as in the word f**a**ther.
> "**v**" is pronounced "**w**" as in the word **w**hale
> "**e**" is pronounced "**eh**" as in the word p**e**t.

If we put the sounds together **ee** + **ah** + **w** + **eh** it produces *Yahweh*. The **ee** sound + **ah** sound = *Yah* and **w** + **eh** = *Weh*. Put the two sounds together and it pronounces *Yahweh* spelled IOVE in classical Latin which is the King of all the Roman Gods, *Jupiter*.[61] The Ancient Romans worshiped and praised the name *Yahweh* sounded exactly as White believes the Sacred Name is pronounced. While similar spelled names in modern English like *jovial* and *by jove* can cause one to assume Jove should be *Joe-vay* and not *Yah-weh*, this goes

---

gleaned the information, that is mostly public domain info anyway, but concise on Avery's Pure Bible Forum, which is mostly a KJV defense site. I have also quoted Ehrman, Wikipedia, Wallace, and others I disagree with. If Avery is anti-Trinitarian, I disagree with him, if he is not, then these accusations are slanderous. Anyquotes from His forum that I have repeated here are mostly linguistic and not theological at all.
[61] http://latindiscussion.com/forum/latin/similarity-of-vocalization-of-iove-and-yahweh.27878/

against the classical Latin pronunciation which can change from culture to culture. Take for example the Italian day of the week Thursday – Giovedì which comes from the Latin Jove dies, or "day of Jove" (aka Jupiter). Giovedi is pronounced Jo-ve-di.

2) Piter = father.

> Jupiter (from Latin: Iūpiter [ˈjuːpɪtɛr] or Iuppiter [ˈjʊppɪtɛr], from Proto-Italic *djous "day, sky" + *patēr "father," thus "heavenly father"), also known as Jove gen. Iovis [ˈjɔwɪs]), is the god of the sky and thunder and king of the gods in Ancient Roman religion and mythology. (Wikipedia)[62]

Thus Jove (Yahweh) + piter = Jupiter. [63]

---

[62] https://en.wikipedia.org/wiki/Jupiter_(mythology) I have shown Wikipedia here to appeal to the lowest bog standard there is which demonstrates a general consensus, not that I am appealing to Wikipedia as a definitive source of infallible information. (These types of disclaimers are needed, because one can be assured that White or other text critics will not address the core issues in this book, but nit pick for unscholarly inconsistencies and genetic fallacy associations.)

[63] (Also from Wikipedia) The Latin name Iuppiter originated as a vocative compound of the Old Latin vocative *Iou and pater ("father") and came to replace the Old Latin nominative case *Ious. Jove is a less common English formation based on Iov-, the stem of oblique cases of the Latin name. Linguistic studies identify the form *Iou-pater as deriving from the Indo-European vocative compound *Dyēu-pəter (meaning "O Father Sky-god"; nominative: *Dyēus-pətēr).

Older forms of the deity's name in Rome were Dieus-pater ("day/sky-father"), then Diéspiter. The 19th-century philologist George Wissowa asserted these names are conceptually- and linguistically-connected to Diovis and Diovis Pater; he compares the analogous formations Vedius-Veiove and fulgur Dium, as opposed to fulgur Summanum (nocturnal lightning bolt) and flamen Dialis (based on Dius, dies). The Ancient later viewed them as entities separate from Jupiter. The terms are similar in etymology and semantics (dies, "daylight" and Dius, "daytime sky"), but differ linguistically. Wissowa considers the epithet Dianus noteworthy. Dieus is the etymological equivalent of ancient Greece's Zeus and of the Teutonics' Ziu (genitive Ziewes). The Indo-European deity is the god from which the names and partially the theology of Jupiter, Zeus and the Indo-Aryan Vedic Dyaus Pita derive or have developed.

The Roman practice of swearing by Jove to witness an oath in law courts is the origin of the expression "by Jove!" —archaic, but still in use. The name of the god was also adopted as the name of the planet Jupiter; the adjective "jovial" originally described those born under the planet of Jupiter (reputed to be jolly, optimistic, and buoyant in temperament).

Thus, James White calls upon the most Sacred Name of God with a name undistinguishable from *Jupiter* and calls him the God of the bible! The second line of "The Lord's Prayer", says, "Hallowed be thy **name**" (Luke 11:2); we are promised that, "Everyone who calls on the **name** of the LORD will be saved" (Romans 10:13); Peter quotes Joel 2:32 in Acts 2:21, "In the last days whosoever calls on the **name** of the Lord shall be saved"; and even a look at the Ten Commandments in Exodus 20:7 "Thou shalt not take the **name** of the LORD thy God in vain; for the LORD will not hold him guiltless that taketh his **name** in vain."

Now, be assured I am not a Sacred Names adherent, and anyone who has read my material on Easter knows that I have thoroughly debunked the etymological pagan Ishtar/Easter link.[64] And I understand that our society has pagan names of the week and months and even our Thursday (Thor's Day) is a calque of Latin dies Iovis (dies Jovis), via an association (Interpretātiō germānica) of the god Thor with the Roman god of thunder Jove (Jupiter). But White is actually calling upon Jupiter as the biblical God saying it is *the* most holy name and saying "Jehovah is a false pronunciation"!

> Ye cannot drink the cup of the Lord, and the cup of devils: ye cannot be partakers of the Lord's table, and of the table of devils. (1 Corinthians 10:21)

While in context communion is the immediate subject, the verse applies perfectly to knowingly calling upon the

---

Jove was the original namesake of Latin forms of the weekday now known in English as Thursday (originally called Iovis Dies in Latin). These became jeudi in French, jueves in Spanish, joi in Romanian, giovedì in Italian, dijous in Catalan, Xoves in Galician, Joibe in Friulian, Dijóu in Provençal.
[64] www.easterau.com

name of a devil or calling our God Jupiter. Remember, no biblical individuals were named after Yahweh. To show how general this is, again the bog standard basics of Wikipedia explains:

> The Hebrew scholar Wilhelm Gesenius [1786–1842] suggested that the Hebrew punctuation יַהְוֶה, which is transliterated into English as *Yahweh*, might more accurately represent the pronunciation of the tetragrammaton than the Biblical Hebrew punctuation "יְהֹוָה", from which the English name Jehovah has been derived. His proposal to read YHWH as "יַהְוֶה" was based in large part on various Greek transcriptions, such as ιαβε[65], dating from the first centuries CE but also on the forms of theophoric names. In his Hebrew Dictionary, Gesenius supports Yahweh (which would have been pronounced [jahwe], with the final letter being silent) because of the Samaritan pronunciation ιαβε reported by Theodoret, and because the theophoric name prefixes YHW [jeho] and YW [jo], the theophoric name suffixes YHW [jahu] and YH [jah], and the abbreviated form YH [jah] can be derived from the form Yahweh.[66] Gesenius's proposal to read YHWH as יַהְוֶה is accepted as the best scholarly reconstructed vocalised Hebrew spelling of the tetragrammaton.[67]

---

[65] While several scholars point to ιαβε being pronounced as *Yahweh*, the Greek here is not a good indication and does not usurp the basic Hebrew. ιαβε may actually have been pronounced as y-ao-ve and sound more like *Yehovah* than *Yahweh* or it may, as I assume, also be in a Nomen Sacrum form described in our latter section on Nomina Sacra. Either way, this should not be a reading that usurps all others.

[66] *A Hebrew and English Lexicon of the Old Testament with an appendix containing the Biblical Aramaic*, written by Francis Brown, Samuel Rolles Driver and Charles Augustus Briggs, based on the Hebrew lexicon of Wilhelm Gesenius as translated by Edward Robinson, Oxford: The Clarendon Press, 1906, s. 218.

[67] Paul Joüon and T. Muraoka. A Grammar of Biblical Hebrew (Subsidia Biblica). Part One: Orthography and Phonetics. Rome: Editrice Pontificio Istituto Biblio, 1996. ISBN 978-8876535956. Quote from Section 16(f)(1)" "The Qre is יְהֹוָה *the Lord*, whilst the Ktiv is probably(1) יַהְוֶה (according to ancient witnesses)." "Note 1: In our translations, we have used *Yahweh*, a form widely accepted by scholars, instead of the traditional *Jehovah*"

So we see that the modern concept of the name *Yahweh* goes back to Gesenius. But not only did Samuel Prideaux Tregelles dispel the *Yahweh* myth but Gesenius himself thoroughly retracted what he wrote about it. Tregelles translated the work of Gesenius into English and the complete transcription is available online.[68] The section Gesenius writes about is written here with interpolations by the translator/editor Tregelles below[69]:

> To give my own opinion [This opinion Gesenius afterwards THOROUGHLY retracted; see Thes. and Amer. trans. in voc.: he calls such comparisons and derivations, "waste of time and labour;" would that he had learned how irreverent a mode this was of treating such subjects!], I suppose this word to be one of the most remote antiquity, perhaps of the same origin as *Jovis, Jupiter,* and transferred from the Egyptians to the Hebrews [What an idea! God himself revealed this as his own name; the Israelites could never have received it from the Egyptians]; (compare what has been said above, as to the use of this name on the Egyptian gems [but these gems are not of the most remote antiquity; they are the work of heretics of the second and third centuries]), and then so inflected by the Hebrews, that it might appear, both in form and origin, to be Phenicio-Shemitic (see מִשְׁנֶה, בְּהֵמוֹת).

This is also written in the footnote below[70]

[68] https://web.archive.org/web/20170327125227/http://www.masseiana.org/gesenius.htm.
[69] https://archive.org/stream/GeseniusHebrewChaldeeLexiconOldTestamentScriptures. tregelles.1857.24/10.GesenHebChalLexOTS.Yod.Tregelles1857.ggle.msft.#page/n11/mode/2up
[70]

Gesenius: To give my own opinion,

   Tregelles: This opinion Gesenius afterwards THOROUGHLY retracted; see Thes. and Amer. trans, in voc.: he calls such comparisons and derivations, "waste of time and labour;" would that he had learned how irreverent a mode this was of treating such subjects!

Gesenius: I suppose this word to be one of the most remote antiquity, perhaps of the same origin as *Jovis, Jupiter,* and transferred from the Egyptians to the Hebrews;

   Tregelles: What an idea! God himself revealed this as his own name; the Israelites could never have received it from the Egyptians

So as we can see Gesenius had very little substance in his argumentation which was merely a conjectural blunder. But he opened up the Egyptian and Latin paganism theories for the name Yahweh. Leonard Ravenhill mentioned in a sermon:

> "In 170 BC there was a man with the strange name of Antiochus Epiphanes. You need to look up his name and his relatives. He took over Jerusalem, he polluted the temple, he made the Jews sacrifice to idols, he built a statue of Jupiter where the altar of the burnt offering should have been. He burnt the Scriptures publicly. He prohibited the worship of Jehovah."[71]

Note, Jupiter replaced Jehovah and worship to Jehovah was forbidden. This issue of replacement will become apparent when we look at the section in this book on commentaries, when the Triadic Declaration was also used for blasphemy: "Jupiter was; Jupiter is; Jupiter shall be."

While Jove, Jehovah, Yahweh, do have *some* phonetic similarities, the bulk of evidence proves *Jehovah* to be the Sacred Name. To defiantly say God is *Yahweh* and inserting the exact equivalent of a pagan god in its place is to deny the biblical and linguistic evidence seen above. James White should humble himself and learn the facts about the Sacred Name before calling it a false

---

Gesenius: (compare what has been said above, as to the use of this name on the Egyptian gems),
> Tregelles: but these gems are not of the most remote antiquity; they are the work of heretics of the second and third centuries
Gesenius: and then so inflected by the Hebrews, that it might appear, both in form and origin, to be Phenicio-Shemitic.

(Extracted from *Gesenius's Hebrew and Chaldee Lexicon to the Old Testament Scriptures,* 1846, pp. CCCXXXVII-VIII.)

https://archive.org/details/GeseniusHebrewChaldeeLexiconOldTestamentScriptures.tregelles.1857.24/page/n3
[71] http://articles.ochristian.com/article581.shtml

pronunciation and demonizing those who call upon It.[72] But as we shall see; these elementary issues are just the tip of the iceberg concerning the ignorance of White on these topics.

1.4 The Father and the Son are both Jehovah

In the list below we can see several traits that Jesus and the Father both have. The entire Godhead is a trinity, meaning that the Father, Son and Spirit, are allpart of the Godhead but in three distinct persons. But to save time, we are only primarily looking at the concept of Jehovah being both Jesus and the Father. Anyone who has ever tried to debate Unitarians, Jehovah's Witnesses, Mormons, or Christadelphians will have studied this concept. This list is not exhaustive, but for the purpose of showing that Jesus is Jehovah the following small list of examples leave us no doubt on the issue. I was tempted to regulate these verses to an appendix, but I think it is good left in the main body of text, to remind us of who the Jehovah "who is to come" and "who shalt be", is.

Jesus and Jehovah are both the **first and the last**:

> I the LORD (Jehovah), **the first, and with the last**; I am he. - Isaiah 41:4.
> Thus saith the LORD (Jehovah) the King of Israel, and his redeemer the LORD (Jehovah) of hosts; **I am the first, and I am the last**; and beside me there is no God.' - Isaiah 44:6.

> I am the **first and the last**: I am he that liveth and was dead. - Revelation 1:17,18

---

[72] Much of this linguistic documentation is from www.purebibleforum.com

Jesus and Jehovah are both the **Alpha and Omega**:

> I am **Alpha and Omega**, the beginning and the ending, saith the Lord,......the Almighty. - Revelation 1:8; 21:5-7.

> I am **Alpha and Omega**, the beginning and the end, the first and the last (v.13)....I Jesus (v16). - Revelation 22:13-16.[73]

Jesus and Jehovah both **do not change**:

> I am the LORD (Jehovah), **I change not**. - Malachi 3:6.

> Jesus Christ **the same**, yesterday, and to day, and for ever. - Hebrews 13:8.

Jesus and Jehovah are **all powerful**:

> I am the **Almighty God**. - Genesis 17:1.
> With God **all things are possible**. - Matthew 19:26.
> There is **nothing too hard** for thee. - Jeremiah 32:17.

> **All power** is given unto me in heaven and in earth. - Matthew 28:18.
> Upholding **all things** by the word of **his power**. - Hebrews 1:3.
> I am Alpha and Omega . . . **the Almighty**. - Revelation 1:8.

Jesus and Jehovah are both **eternal**:

> The **eternal** God is thy refuge. - Deuteronomy 33:27.

> Having **neither beginning of days, nor end of life**; but made like unto the Son of God. - Hebrews 7:3.

---

[73] Note: Watchtower, 1 October 1978, p.15, says this is Jesus.

Also Jehovah the Holy Spirit is **eternal**:

the **eternal** Spirit. - Hebrews 9:14.

Jesus and Jehovah both have an **everlasting kingdom**:

Thy kingdom is an **everlasting kingdom**.
- Psalm 145:13.[74]

Son of man . . . his dominion is **an everlasting dominion**.... and his kingdom that which shall not be destroyed.' - Daniel 7:13, 14.
 The everlasting kingdom of our Lord and Saviour Jesus Christ'. - 2 Peter 1:11.

Jesus and Jehovah both **shall appear**:

When the LORD (Jehovah) shall build up Zion, he **shall appear** in his glory. - Psalm 102:16.

The glorious **appearing** of our great God and our Saviour Jesus Christ. - Titus 2:13.
They shall **look upon me** whom they have pierced. - Zechariah 12:10.

and **every eye shall see him**, and they also which pierced him: - Revelation 1:7

Jesus and Jehovah are both the **Lord of that day**.

The **day of the LORD** (Jehovah) is at hand.
- Isaiah 13:6.

Until **the day** of Jesus Christ. - Philippians 1:6.
...as that **the day** of Christ is at hand.

---

74 Note: Jehovah's kingdom equals Christ's everlasting kingdom.

- 2 Thessalonians 2:2.

Jesus and Jehovah are both **the King**:

> Mine eyes have seen **the King**, the LORD (Jehovah) of hosts. - Isaiah 6:5.
> The LORD (Jehovah) is our **King**. - Isaiah 33:22.

> he (the Lamb) is .... **King** of Kings. - Revelation 17:14.
> Lord Jesus Christ .... who is the blessed and only **Potentate**, the **King** of kings and Lord of lords.
> – 1 Timothy 6:14,15.[75]
> A name written: **KING** OF KINGS and LORD OF LORDS - Revelation 19:16.

Jesus and Jehovah both **destroy the Armies of the earth**:

> The indignation of the LORD (Jehovah) is upon **all nations**, and his fury upon **all their armies**: he hath utterly destroyed them. - Isaiah 34:2.
> Then shall the LORD (Jehovah) go forth and **fight** against **those nations**. - Zechariah 14:3.

> I saw the beast, and the kings of the earth, and **their armies** gathered together to **make war against him** (Jesus Christ) that sat on the horse. - Revelation 19:19.
> In righteousness he doth judge and **make war** (v11). his name is called the Word of God (Jesus Christ) (v.13) the remnant were **slain with the sword of him** (Jesus Christ) that sat upon the horse.' (v 21).
> - Revelation 19:11,13, & 21.

Jesus and Jehovah both **have a voice like many waters**:

---

[75] Note: a Potentate is a monarch or King.

The glory of the God of Israel came.....his voice was **like a noise of many waters**. - Ezekiel 43:2.

His (Christ's) **voice as the sound of many waters**. - Revelation 1:15.

Jesus and Jehovah both have **glory**:

I am the LORD (Jehovah),... My **glory** will I not give to another. - Isaiah 42:8.
God and our Father: to whom **be glory** for ever and ever. Amen. - Galatians 1:4, 5.
To him **be glory** and dominion for ever and ever. – 1 Peter 5:10,11.

Our Lord and Saviour Jesus Christ. To Him **be glory** both now and for ever. Amen. - 2 Peter 3:18.
Jesus Christ; to whom **be glory** for ever and ever. Amen. - Hebrews 13:21.
Jesus Christ, to whom be **praise and dominion** for ever and ever. Amen. 1 Peter 4:11
From Jesus Christ.....to him **be glory** and dominion for ever and ever. Amen. - Revelation 1:5, 6.

Jesus and Jehovah both **will come**:

The LORD (Jehovah) GOD **will come**. - Isaiah 40:10.

Behold, I (Jesus Christ) **come** quickly. - Revelation 22:7, 12, & 20.

Jesus and Jehovah are both **equal**:

All things that the Father hath are mine. - John 16:15. (Including the Name of Jehovah)

That ye also may have fellowship with us: and truly our fellowship is **with the Father, and with his Son Jesus**

Christ. - 1 John 1:3. Both fellowship equally with believers.

Baptising them **in the name of the Father, and of the Son, and of the Holy Ghost** - Matthew 28:19. - Three names have the same level of Authority

Jesus and Jehovah have the **same face**:

The throne of **God and of the Lamb** shall be in it; And they shall see **his face**' - Revelation 22:3, 4.

Jesus and Jehovah have the **same name**:

The throne of God and of the Lamb shall be in it,..... and **his name** shall be in their foreheads.
– Revelation 22:3, 4.

Jesus and Jehovah are both **the temple** of New Jerusalem:

The Lord **God Almighty** and the **Lamb** are the **temple** of it. - Revelation 21:22.

So as we can see from these verses that Jehovah is both the Father and the Son. This is a significant reminder that Jehovah God is the Son of God also. This significance will be revealed in our defense of Revelation 16:5 as we shall see in Theodore Beza's annotations later.

1.5 I AM THAT I AM

Moses was at the Burning Bush when God said to him:

> And God said unto Moses, I AM THAT I AM: and he
> said, Thus shalt thou say unto the children of Israel, I AM
> hath sent me unto you. -Exodus 3:14

Jehovah spoke to Moses in Exodus 3 from the burning
bush and revealed to him His Sacred Name. We have
seen that *Jehovah* and *hava* (to be, become, come to
pass) are connected. But the name Jehovah is also
directly connected to the passage in Exodus 3:14 in
which God gives his name as I AM THAT I AM, or in
Hebrew:

אֶהְיֶה אֲשֶׁר אֶהְיֶה *Ehyah asher Ehyah*

Exodus 3:14 is one of the most famous verses in the
Torah. *Ehyah* means "existed" in Hebrew; *ehyeh* is the
first person singular imperfect form and is usually
translated in English Bibles as "I am" or "I will be" or "I
shall be". The ancient Hebrew of Exodus 3:14 lacks a
future tense, as modern English also does, yet a few
translations render this name as "I Will Be What I Will
Be", in the context of Jehovah promising to be with his
people through their future troubles.

A notable example is the Miles Coverdale Bible of
1535 which has:

> God saide vnto Moses: **I wyl be what I wyll be.** And he
> sayde: Thus shalt thou saye vnto ye children of Israel: I
> **wyl be** hath sent me vnto you .- Exodus 3:14, Coverdale
> Bible

Coverdale's "I wyll be" is the equivalent to Beza's
ἐσόμενος (esomenos), and "shalt be" (will be) in the KJV
in revelation 16:5. So while we have seen that "shalt
be/will be" is clearly part of the Sacred Name of
Jehovah, it is also part of the great I AM. The word
ehyeh is used a total of 43 places in the Hebrew Bible,

where it is often translated as "I will be" such as is the case for its first occurrence, in Genesis 26:3 and its final occurrence in Zechariah 8:8. Notice:

> Sojourn in this land, and **I will be** with thee, and will bless thee; for unto thee, and unto thy seed, I will give all these countries, and I will perform the oath which I sware unto Abraham thy father; - Genesis 26:3 וְאֶהְיֶה waehyah and I will be

> And I will bring them, and they shall dwell in the midst of Jerusalem: and they shall be my people, and **I will be** their God, in truth and in righteousness. - Zechariah 8:8 אֶהְיֶה ehyah I will be

In the Hellenistic Greek literature of the Jewish Diaspora the phrase "Ehyeh asher ehyeh" was rendered in Greek "ego eimi ho on", "I am the being". Aquila and Theodotion both made Greek versions of the Old Testament and translate "ehyeh asher ehyeh" and the single "ehyeh" of Exodus 3:14 into Greek as *esomai hos esomai* and *esomai* respectively, which in turn translates as "I will be who I will be" and "I will be". They chose to replace the words "ego eimi" with "esomai", which is to replace the words "I am" with "I will be", and, in keeping with the apparent intention of the Hebrew text, they translated all three occurrences of "ehyeh" in this way. Victor P. Hamilton suggests:

> "some legitimate translations [...]: (1) 'I am who I am'; (2) 'I am who I was'; (3) 'I am who I shall be'; (4) 'I was who I am'; (5) 'I was who I was'; (6) 'I was who I shall be'; (7) 'I shall be who I am'; (8) 'I shall be who I was'; (9) 'I shall be who I shall be.'"[76]

---

[76] Exodus: An Exegetical Commentary, by Victor P. Hamilton, Page 64, Baker Books, 1 Nov 2011 - 752 pages

Consider these Jewish commentaries on I AM and similar threefold formulas:

'I am he who is and **who will be**' – Exodus 3:14, Targum Pseudo-Jonathan.

'I am now what I always was and **always will be**' - Exodus 3.6, Midrash Rabba; Alphabet of Rabbi Akiba; also Midrash Psalm 72:1.

'I am he who is and who was, and I am he **who will be**' – Deuteronomy 32:39, Targum Pseudo-Jonathan; see also the gloss to Targum, Neofiti Exodus 3:14.

Neofiti's rendering of this *ehyeh* clearly articulates his understanding of its root meaning as 'to be' in the sense of 'to exist'. Targum Pseudo-Jonathan renders *ehyeh asher ehyeh* in similar terms to Neofiti as, "He who said and the world was, (who) said and everything was", which also reveals the concept of the root meaning of *chyeh* as 'to be' in the sense of 'to exist' and of being the creator. Pseudo-Jonathan goes on to render the *ehyeh* of Exodus 3:14 as "I am who I am and **who will be**", revealing the immutability of God. The 10th Century Arabic Saadia's translation (Tafsir) as recorded in the London Polyglot of 1657 has in its Latin paraphrase of Exodus 3:14:

Dixit ei, **Aeturnus**, qui non praeterit,

Translated as,

He said to him, **The Eternal**, who does not pass away.

Moses Mendelssohn states that:

Saadia Gaon writes that the explanation is, "who is not past and **will not pass away**, because He is the first and the last".

From the two, it is evident that Saadia's brief rendering of the verse is a loose paraphrase of the entire verse, in which there is no apparent distinction being made between the declarations of "I am that I am", and simply "I am", and that it is framed in terms of the eternality of God. In the 18th Century, Mendelssohn translated the first Jewish translation of the Bible into High German. It reads in English:

> God spoke to Moses: "I am the being **that is eternal**". He said further: "Say to the children of Israel, '**The eternal being**, which calls itself, **I-am-eternal**, has sent me to you.

Jewish critics of Mendelssohn's Bible Martin Buber and Franz Rosenzweig, went on to produce a German translation of their own. It says at Exodus 3:14:

> God said to Moshe: **I will be-there** howsoever **I will be-there**. And He said: Thus shall you say to the Sons of Israel: **I-Will-Be-There** sends me to you.

The first Jewish translation into English was the 1917 Jewish Publication Society Bible, which reads exactly as the KJV with:

> And God said unto Moses: '**I AM THAT I AM**'; and He said: 'Thus shalt thou say unto the children of Israel: **I AM** hath sent me unto you'.

The ArtScroll Tanakh, a non-literal translation especially popular amongst more traditional and Orthodox Jews corresponds with the translations of Aquila and Theodotion, and reads:

Hashem answered Moses, "**I Shall Be** As **I Shall Be**." And He said, "So you shall say to the Children of Israel, '**I Shall Be** has sent me to you'". Hashem = Sacred Name, i.e. Jehovah.

Similarly in William Propp's 1998 translation of Exodus in The Anchor Bible series it has:

Then Deity said to Moses, "**I will be** who **I will be**". And He said, "Thus you will say to Israel's Sons: '**I-will-be**' has sent me to you'".

From the above it is clear that, Jewish Bible translations from many sources translate Exodus 3:14 as "shall be" or "will be" which is the exact way that Beza has it in Revelation 16:5. This link will become more apparent in latter chapters when we look at the external evidence for Revelation 16:5 in Church writings and language bible versions.

1.6 I AM in English bible versions

A simple examination of the various English versions of Exodus 3:14 shows us that "I AM" has various meaning among bible translations. The King James is the most accurate translation of the English bible with "I AM", with "AM" covering all aspects of past, present, and future. Jehovah simply is. An atheist might ask a believer, "where did God come from" and a usual response could be that "God always was, always is, and always will be." He simply just IS. Hebrews 11:6 states:

But without faith it is impossible to please him: for he that cometh to God must believe that **he is**, and that he is a rewarder of them that diligently seek him.

While many of these below versions are actually perversions of God's word in several places, may be based upon poor manuscripts, and may be produced by unregenerate translators, this demonstration clearly shows us that "I AM" has several distinct meanings that relate to the reading in Revelation 16:5. The vast majority of English versions simply say "I AM that I AM", or "I am who I am", with the latter "I AM" in Exodus 3:14, so I have left most of those common versions out here and have focused upon exceptions and variances to that standard reading:

> The Lord seide to Moises, **Y am that am**. The Lord seide, Thus thou schalt seie to the sones of Israel, **He that is** sente me to you. - Wycliffe Bible 1395

> God saide vnto Moses: **I wyl be what I wyll be**. And he sayde: Thus shalt thou saye vnto ye children of Israel: **I wyl be** hath sent me vnto you. - Coverdale Bible 1535

> God replied, "**I AM THE ONE WHO ALWAYS IS**. Just tell them, '**I AM** has sent me to you.'" - New Living Translation

> And God said to Moses, **I AM WHO I AM and WHAT I AM, and I WILL BE WHAT I WILL BE**; and He said, You shall say this to the Israelites: **I AM** has sent me to you! - The Amplified Bible

> God said to Moses: **I am the eternal God**. So tell them that **the LORD**, whose name is "**I Am**," has sent you. This is my name forever, and it is the name that people must use from now on. - Contemporary English Version

> God said to Moses, "**I am who I am**.[c] This is what you are to say to the Israelites: '**I am** has sent me to you.'" - New International Version Footnote a. Exodus 3:14 Or **I will be what I will be**

And God saith unto Moses, `**I AM THAT WHICH I AM**;' He saith also, `Thus dost thou say to the sons of Israel, **I AM** hath sent me unto you.' - Young's Literal Translation

And God said unto Moses, **I Will Become whatsoever I please**, And he said- Thus, shalt thou say to the sons of Israel, **I Will Become** hath sent me unto you. - The Emphasised Bible

God said to Moshe, "**Ehyeh Asher Ehyeh [I am/will be what I am/will be]**," and added, "Here is what to say to the people of Isra'el: **'Ehyeh [I Am or I Will Be]** has sent me to you.'" - The Complete Jewish Bible

And God answered unto Moses, **I AM THAT I AM**. And he said, Thus shalt thou say unto the sons of Israel: **I AM (YHWH)** has sent me unto you. Jubilee Bible 2000

And Elohim said unto Moshe, **Eh-heh-yeh ashair Ehheh- yeh (I AM WHO I AM)**; and He said, Thus shalt thou say unto the Bnei Yisroel, **EHHEH-YEH (I AM)** hath sent me unto you. Orthodox Jewish Bible

1.7 Before Abraham was I AM

The very name of Jesus means "Jehovah is salvation". Joshua (Yeshua or Yehoshua with the "eh" sound) was a common biblical name. Those who penned the New Testament used Ἰησοῦς (ee-ay-sooce) for Jesus. The Anglicized Jesus is derived from the Latin Iesus. In scripture Jesus is clearly Jehovah. Both the Father and Son are called Jehovah, and attributes of the Father are also identical to the Son. But Jesus is clearly the "I AM" of Exodus 3:14 also. John, who also wrote Revelation 16:5, clearly saw the connection of Christ being the "I

AM" in his gospel. Jesus was constantly name dropping the "I AM":

> Verily, verily, I say unto you, Before Abraham was, **I AM**.
> - John 8:58.

After Jesus said this, the Jews took stones to cast them upon Him because He said that God was His Father, making Himself equal with God (John 5:18).[77] They wanted to stone Him because by saying "I AM" Jesus had claimed that Sacred Name of Exodus 3:14 for Himself:

> Before Abraham was, **I AM**. - John 8:58.

This very same "I AM" who spoke to Moses out of the bush, who later descended in front of Moses in a cloud, and proclaimed the name of the Lord (Exodus 34), was standing right in front of them. In John 18:4-8 when they came to arrest Jesus, He asked them:

> Whom seek ye? They answered him, Jesus of Nazareth. Jesus saith unto them, **I am *he***.... As soon then as he had said unto them, **I am *he***, they went backward, and fell to the ground. Then asked he them again, Whom seek ye? And they said, Jesus of Nazareth. Jesus answered, I have told you that **I am *he***: if therefore ye seek me, let these go their way... (Italics original)

Notice the italic in the phrase "I am *he*". The strict reading is "I AM", but this pattern is in many verses and it would be foolish to translate each instance that way, as it would disturb the narrative and also Jesus was

---

[77] Amazingly, most modern versions butcher Phil 2:6 By claiming that Jesus "did not consider equality with God a thing to be grasped." But Jesus clearly did claim to be equal with God and claimed to be the I AM. Even unspiritual Jews whom Jesus called "sons of the devil" could see when Jesus was claiming to be equal with God. It seems the modern version translators in Phil 2:6 Cannot see such things and thus create a contradiction.

constantly using such allegories. Notice that they went backward and fell to the ground. Perhaps these soldiers knew the truth, that this Man was the Almighty I AM but were obligated under orders to arrest him. This is not a pseudo Charismatic "slain in the spirit" moment, but a natural reaction of someone confronted with the I AM. Jesus also called Himself "I AM" when talking with the Samaritan woman.

> Jesus saith unto her, **I** that speak unto thee **am** he. – John 4:26

The original Greek says **Ἐγὼ εἰμι**, ὁ λαλῶν σοι, "I AM that speaks to thee." After Jesus said this she left her waterpot and went her way back to the city. The "I AM" had spoken to her. In John 6:20 and 8:28 we find Him using the same "I AM" formula again. In the former passage "It is I" can strictly read "I AM." Beside these veiled passages in which He speaks of Himself as the self-existing Jehovah and the great "I AM," Jesus directly reveals seven times in John's Gospel exactly who and what He is to His people:

> I am the Bread of life (6:35.)
> I am the Light of the world (9:5).
> I am the Door (10:7).
> I am the Good Shepherd (10:11).
> I am the Resurrection and the Life (11:25).
> I am the Way, the Truth and the Life (14:6);
> I am the true Vine (15:1).

Amazingly, these were all written in John's Gospel who also authored Revelation 16:5. In the Old Testament there are seven significant Jehovic names of the "I AM" (It has been said that Psalm 23 incorporates every aspect of these characteristics below):

Jehovah-Jireh: the Lord provides. The lamb provided (Genesis 22).
Jehovah-Rophecah: I am the Lord that healeth thee (Exodus 15).
Jehovah-Nissi: The Lord is my banner, He giveth the Victory (Exodus 17).
Jehovah-Shalom: The Lord is Peace. He is our Peace (Judges 6).
Jehovah-Roi: The Lord is my shepherd, I shall not want (Psalm 23).
Jehovah-Tsidkenu: The Lord is our righteousness (Jeremiah 23).
Jehovah-Shammah: The Lord is there (Ezekiel 48)

Jay Green in his 1976 Green's Literal Translation he explains why he capitalized these sections, and also interprets I AM as Jehovah:

> In translating the Greek words for "I am" in certain places, we have capitalized these words: viz. I AM (see John 8:59 and other places). It is our firm conviction that in those cases Jesus is identifying Himself as Jehovah (Jehovah properly translated meaning, I AM THAT I AM). Jesus is of course the English name assigned to a word which means Jehovah is salvation.

This quotation of Green sums up our first chapter nicely, Jehovah is the I AM, Jehovah is Jesus; Jesus is Jehovah, Jesus is the I AM. The significance of this link to Revelation 16:5 will become more apparent in the next chapter as we examine how Jehovah, translated in Greek as Kurios, becomes the key noun mentioned for triggering the pronouncement of the Triadic Declaration by heavenly beings.

CHAPTER 2

And God said moreover unto Moses, Thus shalt thou say unto the children of Israel, **The LORD** (Jehovah) God of your fathers, the God of Abraham, the God of Isaac, and the God of Jacob, hath sent me unto you: **this is my name for ever**, and this is my memorial unto all generations. - Exodus 3:15

2.1 THE TRIADIC DECLARATION

In this section we will examine the relationship between the Sacred Name Jehovah, the I AM, the five Triadic Declarations in the book of Revelation, such Triadic Declarations from a Hebrew mindset, and other such triadic verses.

The name John is a theophoric name originating from the Hebrew name יוֹחָנָן (Yôḥānān), or in its longer form יְהוֹחָנָן (Yəhôḥānān), meaning "Jehovah has been gracious", so John would have been intimately acquainted with the Sacred Name, knowing its meaning and significance. We have seen that in John's writings that he had a fixation with Jesus being the I AM, but we can also see his infatuation with the name Jehovah expressed in the Triadic Declaration in Revelation. Not that this is John's design or concept, but he simply wrote what he heard and saw. In King James Version the five verses containing the Triadic Declaration translate as:

John to the seven churches which are in Asia: Grace be unto you, and peace, from him **which is, and which was, and which is to come**; and from the seven Spirits which are before his throne; And from Jesus Christ - Revelation 1:4-5

I am Alpha and Omega, the beginning and the ending, saith the Lord, **which is, and which was, and which is to come,** the Almighty. - Revelation 1:8

And the four beasts had each of them six wings about him; and they were full of eyes within: and they rest not day and night, saying, Holy, holy, holy, Lord God Almighty, **which was, and is, and is to come.** - Revelation 4:8

Saying, We give thee thanks, O Lord God Almighty, **which art, and wast, and art to come**; because thou hast taken to thee thy great power, and hast reigned. - Revelation 11:17

And I heard the angel of the waters say, Thou art righteous, O Lord, **which art, and wast, and shalt be,** because thou hast judged thus. - Revelation 16:5

The Triadic Declaration occurs five times in the 1598 Greek Textus Receptus of Beza, all in Revelation as follows:

Ἰωάννης ταῖς ἑπτὰ ἐκκλησίαις ταῖς ἐν τῇ Ἀσίᾳ· χάρις ὑμῖν καὶ εἰρήνη ἀπὸ τοῦ **Ὁ ὢν καὶ Ὁ ἦν καὶ Ὁ ἐρχόμενος**· καὶ ἀπὸ τῶν ἑπτὰ πνευμάτων ἃ ἐστιν ἐνώπιον τοῦ θρόνου αὐτοῦ· καὶ ἀπὸ Ἰησοῦ Χριστοῦ - Revelation 1:4

Ἐγώ εἰμι τὸ Α καὶ τὸ Ω, ἀρχὴ καὶ τέλος, λέγει ὁ Κύριος, **ὁ ὢν καὶ ὁ ἦν καὶ ὁ ἐρχόμενος**, ὁ παντοκράτωρ. - Revelation 1:8

58

Καὶ τέσσαρα ζῷα, ἓν καθ' ἑαυτὸ εἶχον ἀνὰ πτέρυγας ἓξ κυκλόθεν, καὶ ἔσωθεν γέμοντα ὀφθαλμῶν· καὶ ἀνάπαυσιν οὐκ ἔχουσιν ἡμέρας καὶ νυκτὸς, λέγοντα, Ἅγιος, ἅγιος, ἅγιος Κύριος ὁ θεὸς ὁ παντοκράτωρ, **Ὁ ἦν καὶ Ὁ ὢν καὶ ἐρχόμενος**. - Revelation 4:8

Λέγοντες, Εὐχαριστοῦμέν σοι, Κύριε ὁ θεὸς ὁ παντοκράτωρ, **Ὁ ὢν, καὶ ὁ ἦν, καὶ Ὁ ἐρχόμενος**· ὅτι εἴληφας τὴν δύναμίν σου τὴν μεγάλην, καὶ ἐβασίλευσας· - Revelation 11:17

Καὶ ἤκουσα τοῦ ἀγγέλου τῶν ὑδάτων λέγοντος, Δίκαιος, Κύριε, εἶ **Ὁ ὢν, καὶ Ὁ ἦν, καὶ ὁ ἐσόμενος**, ὅτι ταῦτα ἔκρινας. - Revelation 16:5

The phrase ὁ ὢν καὶ ὁ ἦν καὶ ὁ ἐρχόμενος/ἐσόμενος is directly related to the eternal name of God. In fact, Strong in his Greek dictionary definitions gives the entire Triadic Declaration its own Strong's number and Spiros Zodhiates has two and a half pages on this one Strong's number. Strong has:[78]

---

[78] **3801 ὁ ὢν καί ὁ ἦν καί ὁ ἐρχόμενος**
(ho ṑn kaí ho ēn kaí ho erchómenos, ho own kahee ho ane kahee ho er-khom'-en-os);
a phrase combining G3588 with the present participle and imperfect of G1510 and the present participle of G2064 by means of G2532; the one being and the one that was and the one coming, i.e. the Eternal, as a divine epithet of Christ:—which art (is, was), and (which) wast (is, was), and art (is) to come (shalt be).

1890 Strong's Concordance - *The Exhaustive Concordance of the Bible: Showing Every Word of the Text of the Common English Version of the Canonical Books, and Every Occurrence of Each Word in Regular Order: Together with A Comparative Concordance of the Authorized and Revised Versions, Including the American Variations; Also Brief Dictionaries of the Hebrew and Greek Words of the Original, with References to the English Words*

3801. ὁ ὢν καί ὁ ἦν καί ὁ ἐρχόμενος **hŏ ōn kaí hŏ ēn kaí hŏ ĕrchŏmĕnŏs**, *hŏ own kahee hŏ ane kahee hŏ er-khom'-en-os;* a phrase combining *3588* with the pres. part. and imperf. of *1510* and the pres. part. of *2064* by means of *2532; the one being and the one that was and the one coming,* i.e. *the Eternal,* as a divine epithet of Christ:—**which art (is, was), and (which) wast (is, was), and art (is) to come (shalt be).**

Take notice that what Strong is showing here is that the English Triadic Declaration "which art (is, was), and (which) wast (is, was), and art (is) to come (**shalt be**)", fits into a single Strong's Greek definition entry (3801). This is because the entire phrase is *nominative*, i.e. a name, a divine title, an expansion of the Jehovah and I AM. This is called a *noun phrase* the words involved are called a *nominal group*:

> which is, and which was, and which is to come
> which is, and which was, and which is to come
> which was, and is, and is to come
> which art, and wast, and art to come
> which art, and wast, and shalt be

The pattern of the Triadic Declaration can be seen even clearer in Greek:

ὁ	ὢν	καὶ	ὁ	ἦν	καὶ	ὁ	ἐρχόμενος	Rev 1:4
ὁ	ὢν	καὶ	ὁ	ἦν	καὶ	ὁ	ἐρχόμενος	Rev 1:8
ὁ	ἦν	καὶ	ὁ	ὢν	καὶ	ὁ	ἐρχόμενος	Rev 4:8
ὁ	ὢν	καὶ	ὁ	ἦν	καὶ	ὁ	ἐρχόμενος	Rev 11:17
ὁ	ὢν	καὶ	ὁ	ἦν	καὶ	ὁ	ἐσόμενος	Rev 16:5

2.2 The Triadic Declaration and Jehovah

There is a notable link to the Triadic Declaration and Jehovah. On close examination, the "Lord" (*Kurios*) is mentioned around these verses which could simply be back-translated into Hebrew as Jehovah from John's perspective. In the five instances of the Triadic Declaration, Jehovah is close by, but the latter four are more distinct, as Jehovah is not *specifically* mentioned in 1:4-5. Thus, this first instance deviates slightly from the pattern of the latter four. I personally think that John being the human instrument that God used to bring His words to us, was simply parroting the Triadic Declaration in his introduction to Revelation, due to his frequent hearing of it being spoken by the heavenly eternal beings in the visions he saw and heard.

Yet, another possibility is that the name Jesus in 1:5 had already been defined as Jehovah according to John's gospel and other writings, and thus would suffice to claim that Jehovah is there and the mention of Jesus simply is akin to saying Jehovah. Another angle, is that Jesus' name is Jehoshua, and thus Jehovah does appear in the details of His name also. Another possibility is that in this first instance, all members of the *Trinity* are present, and thus the threefold *Jehovah* is also. John mentions: *Him, Seven Spirits, and Jesus Christ*; the entire *Jehovah* the trinity is mentioned.

But as mentioned above, I think it is because John was *earthy* and simply parroted what he had heard from the other four mentions which are of *heavenly* origin. This is Johns only mention of the Triadic Declaration in his own words, and each other instance John is quoting someone else. John said:

> Revelation 1:4-5 John to the seven churches which are in Asia: Grace be unto you, and peace, from **him** which is, and which was, and which is to come; and from the

seven Spirits which are before his throne; And from **Jesus Christ**...

Each other time after chapter 1 verse 4, the word "Lord" (*Jehovah*) appears when the Triadic Declaration does. Below I have put the Hebrew name *Jehovah* into these verses in place of *Lord* just so we can clearly see the link between the Triadic Declaration and Jehovah:

> I am Alpha and Omega, the beginning and the ending, saith the **Jehovah, which is, and which was, and which is to come**, the Almighty. - Revelation 1:8

> And the four beasts had each of them six wings about him; and they were full of eyes within: and they rest not day and night, saying, Holy, holy, holy, **Jehovah** God Almighty, **which was, and is, and is to come**. - Revelation 4:8

> Saying, We give thee thanks, O **Jehovah** God Almighty, **which art, and wast, and art to come**; because thou hast taken to thee thy great power, and hast reigned. - Revelation 11:17

> And I heard the angel of the waters say, Thou art righteous, **O Jehovah, which art, and wast, and shalt be**, because thou hast judged thus. - Revelation 16:5

So while we can see then that Revelation 1:8 is a quote from Jesus, 4:8 is from the four living creatures, 11:17 is from the 24 elders (of v.16) and the final in 16:5 is from the angel of the waters. It is interesting that in chapter 16 in context, the person from the alter echoes what the other third angel said. I have also placed Jehovah in place of Lord here:

> 5 And I heard the angel of the waters say, Thou art righteous, **O Jehovah, which art, and wast, and shalt be,** because thou hast judged thus.

6 For they have shed the blood of saints and prophets, and thou hast given them blood to drink; for they are worthy.

7 And I heard **another** out of the altar say, Even so, **Jehovah** God Almighty, true and righteous are thy judgments.[79] – Revelation 16:5-7

At first, the significance of this may not be clearly seen, but when one looks into how many times "Lord" is declared in Revelation, it becomes evident that the Triadic Declaration and Lord *Jehovah* are intimately linked here.

Below is a list of every time the word Lord (kurios) appears in Revelation. We can see from the context that in every instance of the word Lord before the instance of the second coming of Jesus, is speaking about the Triadic Declaration. There are other things like prayers, and basic dialogue, but it is certain that John is linking Jehovah with the phrase. Of course chronologically, once Christ returns, the "is to come" and "shalt be" would become simply "is". Examine the verses below in context:

A clear link to Jehovah:

I am Alpha and Omega, the beginning and the ending, saith the **Lord**, **which is, and which was, and which is to come, the Almighty**. - Revelation 1:8

This is simply narrative and dialogue:

I was in the Spirit on the **Lord's** day, and heard behind me a great voice, as of a trumpet, - Revelation 1:10

---

[79] This is significant also, because the other out of the alter says Jehovah, which was an echo of 16:5. The critical text omits the *Lord* (Greek Kurios, Hebrew Jehovah) from 16:5, causing the other being to parrot a name apparently not there in the first place. This demonstrates the confusion caused by the critical text.

A clear link to Jehovah:

> And the four beasts had each of them six wings about him; and they were full of eyes within: and they rest not day and night, saying, Holy, holy, holy, **Lord** God Almighty, **which was, and is, and is to come**. And when those beasts give glory and honour and thanks to him that sat on the throne, who liveth for ever and ever, The four and twenty elders fall down before him that sat on the throne, and worship him that liveth for ever and ever, and cast their crowns before the throne, saying, Thou art worthy, O **Lord**, to receive glory and honour and power: for thou hast created all things, and for thy pleasure they are and were created. - Revelation 4:8-11

People simply speaking/praying to God:

> And they cried with a loud voice, saying, How long, O **Lord**, holy and true, dost thou not judge and avenge our blood on them that dwell on the earth? - Revelation 6:10

This is simply narrative and dialogue:

> And their dead bodies shall lie in the street of the great city, which spiritually is called Sodom and Egypt, where also our **Lord** was crucified. - Revelation 11:8

A clear link to Jehovah:

> And the seventh angel sounded; and there were great voices in heaven, saying, The kingdoms of this world are become the kingdoms of our **Lord**, and of his Christ; and he shall reign for ever and ever. And the four and twenty elders, which sat before God on their seats, fell upon their faces, and worshipped God, Saying, We give thee thanks, O **Lord** God Almighty, **which art, and wast, and art to come**; because thou hast taken to thee thy great power, and hast reigned. - Revelation 11:15-17

This is simply narrative and dialogue:

> And I heard a voice from heaven saying unto me, Write, Blessed are the dead which die in the **Lord** from henceforth: Yea, saith the Spirit, that they may rest from their labours; and their works do follow them. - Revelation 14:13

This is a specific song with no room for amplification or Triadic Declarations:

> And they sing the song of Moses the servant of God, and the song of the Lamb, saying, Great and marvellous are thy works, **Lord** God Almighty; just and true are thy ways, thou King of saints. Who shall not fear thee, O **Lord**, and glorify thy name? for thou only art holy: for all nations shall come and worship before thee; for thy judgments are made manifest. - Revelation 15:3-4

A clear link to Jehovah:

> And I heard the angel of the waters say, Thou art righteous, O **Lord, which art, and wast, and shalt be**, because thou hast judged thus. For they have shed the blood of saints and prophets, and thou hast given them blood to drink; for they are worthy. And I heard another out of the altar say, Even so, **Lord** God Almighty, true and righteous are thy judgments. - Revelation 16:5-7

This is simply narrative and dialogue:

> These shall make war with the Lamb, and the Lamb shall overcome them: for he is **Lord** of lords, and King of kings: and they that are with him are called, and chosen, and faithful. - Revelation 17:14

This is simply narrative and dialogue:

Therefore shall her plagues come in one day, death, and mourning, and famine; and she shall be utterly burned with fire: for strong is the **Lord** God who judgeth her. - Revelation 18:8

All of the following verses are in the context after the second coming of Jesus has arrived and so because the ἐρχόμενος (is to come) is and ἐσόμενος (shalt be) has finally arrived they do not imply the future reading. Thus these verses are not applicable to our study, but are merely here to show every verse in Revelation containing Lord.

And after these things I heard a great voice of much people in heaven, saying, **Alleluia**; Salvation, and glory, and honour, and power, unto the **Lord** our God: - Revelation 19:1

And I heard as it were the voice of a great multitude, and as the voice of many waters, and as the voice of mighty thunderings, saying, **Allelula**: for the **Lord** God omnipotent reigneth. - Revelation 19:6

And he hath on his vesture and on his thigh a name written, KING OF KINGS, AND **LORD** OF LORDS. - Revelation 19:16

And I saw no temple therein: for the **Lord** God Almighty and the Lamb are the temple of it. - Revelation 21:22

And there shall be no night there; and they need no candle, neither light of the sun; for the **Lord** God giveth them light: and they shall reign for ever and ever. - Revelation 22:5

And he said unto me, These sayings are faithful and true: and the **Lord** God of the holy prophets sent his angel to shew unto his servants the things which must shortly be done. - Revelation 22:6

He which testifieth these things saith, Surely I come quickly. Amen. Even so, come, **Lord** Jesus. - Revelation 22:20

The grace of our **Lord** Jesus Christ be with you all. Amen. - Revelation 22:21

So an overview of Revelation looking at the word Lord reveals to us that the Triadic Declaration is linked to Jehovah in the details. One must conclude that Jehovah *is* the Triadic Declaration. The complete threefold clause is a reflection of Exodus 3:14. To a Hebrew speaker like John, the link between Jehovah and the Triadic Declaration is elementary, just as I AM is linked to Jesus in his gospel. [80] Why we examined this concept will be further explained as we get to the footnotes of Theodore Beza in later chapters.

2.3 The Triadic Declaration in Hebrew

Edenics is the study which concludes that God spoke Hebrew in the beginning. Until Babel, Hebrew was the original language for everyone. This was also a major

---

[80] James White in 2019 after a minimal Twitter conversation said this about the concept above:

> "The reality is that when Kurios appears....I can show you other places where Kurios appears in revelation where is not followed by the Triadic Formulae. So I don't know what he (Sayers) has in mind here, but that is the assertion being made. It sounds good. If you wanna believe it." (Streamed live on 4 Jan 2019 - https://www.youtube.com/watch?v=yoxQHN_iTJQ From 31:50)

If white had simply humbled himself and read my first draft article he refused to take, he would have seen that I went into detail to explain each instance. But he has no interest in that, but simply wants to regurgitate his own concepts, and misrepresent what I clearly said about this issue.

concept in the Reformation period. Thus in historical context, it would be practical for us to conclude that the Hebrew is spoken in heaven, and thus the angel speaking in Hebrew said:

אֲשֶׁר הָיָה וַאֲשֶׁר הֹוֶה וַאֲשֶׁר יִחְיֶה

Translated as:

"which art, and wast, and shalt be" - Revelation 16:5

The *Hutter Dodecaglott Bible* also known as *The Nuremberg Polyglot* was the work of legendary linguist Elias Hutter who produced the New Testament polyglot in twelve languages. Elias Hutter had previously published a Hebrew Old Testament in 1587. In 1599 he completed his translation of the New Testament in twelve languages: English, French, Italian, Spanish, Polish, Danish, German, Bohemian (a Czech dialect), Latin, Greek, Syriac and Hebrew. This is recognized by scholars as *the* study New Testament. It is also one of the rarest items in bibliography.

The Syriac section of the 1599 was taken from Tremellius's second edition, printed in 1569, with certain additions by Hutter. Seeing Tremellius did not have a translation of the Syriac for Revelation, but rather used Theodore Beza's Greek-Latin text, Hutter may have worked on the Syriac of Revelation himself. The Hebrew was Hutter's own translation. Hutter then went on to the works of publishing the Old Testament in six languages, which he had previously formulated, with the basic grammars and lexicons. The sextuple editions of the Old Testament were printed at Nuremberg in 1599 in folio, but were never finished, being carried no further than the book of Ruth. He was also working on yet another New Testament in twelve more languages, viz., Arabic, Ethiopic, Moscovitic, Hungaric, etc.

Below is Hutter's 12 language Bible at Revelation 16:5:

Revelation 16:5 in The Hutter Dodecaglott

The five verses below are from Hutter's 12 language Polyglot of 1599 which all contain the Triadic Declaration. Yes, Hutter in his *Hebrew* rejects holy for יִהְיֶה which means "shalt be". I have underlined the Triadic Declaration with a thick black line, and excluding the first one where John speaks of the entire Trinity Jehovah (being the only one not mentioned by a heavenly being), the other four have a thin line indicating where Jehovah is in the text. When one compares the Triadic Declaration in Hebrew, the link to "Jehovah" and the "I AM" can be clearly seen.

Also the former list in which we looked at, where Jehovah appears in the context of the Triadic Declaration, is more clearly revealed in these verses:

69

4 יוֹחָנָן לְשֶׁבַע קְהִלֹּת שֶׁהֵן
בְּאַסְיָה תְּחִנָּה לָכֶם וְשָׁלוֹם
מֵאֲשֶׁר הֹוֶה וְהָיָה וְיִהְיֶה וּמִשֶּׁבַע
רוּחוֹת אֲשֶׁר הֵן לִפְנֵי כִסְאוֹ :

Revelation 1:4

מֵאֲשֶׁר הֹוֶה וְהָיָה וְיִהְיֶה

8 אֲנִי הוּא אָלֶף וְתָו רִאשׁוֹן
וְאַחֲרוֹן אָמַר יְהֹוָה אֲשֶׁר הֹוֶה
וַאֲשֶׁר הָיָה וַאֲשֶׁר יִהְיֶה כֹּל יָכוֹל:

Revelation 1:8

אֲשֶׁר הֹוֶה וַאֲשֶׁר הָיָה וַאֲשֶׁר יִהְיֶה

8 וְאַרְבַּע חַיּוֹת שֵׁשׁ כְּנָפַיִם
וְשֵׁשׁ כְּנָפַיִם לְאֶחָת מִסָּבִיב
וּמֵחוּץ מְלֵאוֹת עֵינַיִם וּמְנוּחָה
לֹא יֵשׁ—לָהֶם יוֹמָם וְלָיְלָה
לֵאמֹר קָדוֹשׁ קָדוֹשׁ קָדוֹשׁ יְהֹוָה
צְבָאוֹת כָּל־יָכוֹל אֲשֶׁר הָיָה וְהֹוֶה
וְיִהְיֶה :

Revelation 4:8

אֲשֶׁר הָיָה וְהֹוֶה וְיִהְיֶה

70

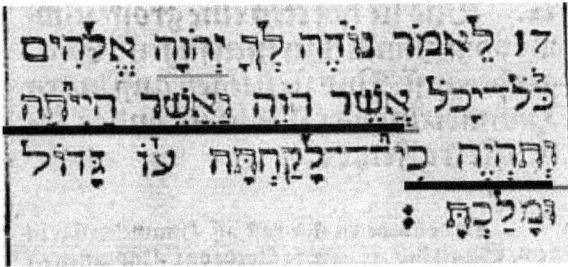

Revelation 11:17

אֲשֶׁר הֹוֶה וַאֲשֶׁר הָיִּחָה וְחֹהְיֶה

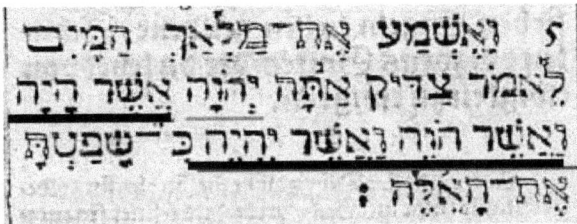

Revelation 16:5

אֲשֶׁר הָיָה וַאֲשֶׁר הֹוֶה וַאֲשֶׁר יֶהְיֶה

Notice in Revelation 16:5 that Hutter has יֶהְיֶה (yihey) and not וְהַסְיָא (holy) in his Hebrew. The Hebrew *yihyeh* means "shalt be", which is Beza's exact reading[81].

The triadic pattern can clearly be seen below. Remember this is most likely how Hebrew speaking John would have heard these verses.

Here is exactly how Hutter has it:

---

[81] http://biblehub.com/hebrew/yihyeh_1961.htm

וְיִהְיֶה		וְהָיָה		הֹוֶה	מֵאֲשֶׁר	Rev 1:4
יִהְיֶה	וַאֲשֶׁר	הָיָה	וַאֲשֶׁר	הֹוֶה	אֲשֶׁר	Rev 1:8
וְיִהְיֶה		וְהָיָה		הָיָה	אֲשֶׁר	Rev 4:8
וְחִהְיֶה		הָיְתָה	וַאֲשֶׁר	הֹוֶה	אֲשֶׁר	Rev 11:17
הִיּה	וַאֲשֶׁר	הֹוֶה	וַאֲשֶׁר	הָיָה	אֲשֶׁר	Rev 16:5

I put space between some prefix letters to show the words clearer in sequence:

הָיֶה			וְי	הָיָה		ו	הֹוֶה	אֲשֶׁר	מ	Rev 1:4
הָיֶה	יְ	אֲשֶׁר	ו	הָיָה	אֲשֶׁר	ו	הֹוֶה	אֲשֶׁר		Rev 1:8
הָיֶה			וְי	הָיָה		ו	הָיָה	אֲשֶׁר		Rev 4:8
הָיֶה	וְח		הָיְתָה	הָי	אֲשֶׁר	ו	הֹוֶה	אֲשֶׁר		Rev 11:17
הָיֶה	יְ	אֲשֶׁר	ו	הֹוֶה	אֲשֶׁר	ו	הָיָה	אֲשֶׁר		Rev 16:5

Notice the link to I AM here: אֶהְיֶה אֲשֶׁר אֶהְיֶה *Ehyah asher Ehyah* consists of אֶ - הְיֶה אֲשֶׁר - אֶ - הְיֶה whereas Revelation 16:5 here is אֲשֶׁר הָיָח וַאֲשֶׁר הֹוֶה וַאֲשֶׁר יִחְיֶה

The יִחְיֶה of Revelation 16:5 still means "to be" even in todays modern Hebrew of יחיה without the vowels.[82] The etymological links to Jehovah's *hava* and *hayah* can be clearly seen here. Interestingly the modern Hebrew also translates אֶהְיֶה *Ehyah* as "I AM" in Hebrew in Exodus 3:14 as "will be". [83]

We can also see from the examples below that Hutter would also use Jehovah for Jesus in his Hebrew New

[82] https://translate.google.com.pk/#iw/en/%D7%99%D7%97%D7%99%D7%97
[83] https://translate.google.com.pk/#auto/en/%D7%90%D7%94%D7%99%D7%94

Testament. For example, in 2 Timothy 1:18 Jehovah is used of Jesus:

יִתֵּן לוֹ יְהוָֹה לִמְצֹא חֵן בְּעֵינֵי 18
יְהוָֹה בַּיּוֹם הַהוּא וְכַמָּה שֵׁרֵת
בְּאֶפְסוֹס אַתָּ הֵיטֵב יָדָעְתָּ ׃

The Lord (Jehovah) grant unto him that he may find mercy of the Lord (Jehovah) in that day...

Likewise, 1 Peter 3:15 has:

וְאֶת־יְהוָֹה אֱלֹהִים אֶת־ 15
הַמָּשִׁיחַ קַדְּשׁוּ בִּלְבַבְכֶם וִהְיִיתֶם
נְכוֹנִים תָּמִיד לְהָשִׁיב דָּבָר לְכָל־
אֲשֶׁר יִשְׁאַל מִכֶּם טַעַם עַל־
אֱמוּנַתְכֶם ׃

But sanctify the Lord (Jehovah) God in your hearts...

Hutter again calls Jehovah Jesus in Acts 9:5:

וַיֹּאמֶר מִי אַתָּ אֲדֹנָי וַיהוָֹה 5
אָמַר אֲנִי יֵשׁוּעַ אֲשֶׁר תִּרְדְּפֵנוּ
יִקְשֶׁה לְךָ לִבְעֹט עַל־הַדָּרְבָּן ׃

And he said, Who art thou, Lord (Adonai)? And the Lord (Jehovah) said, I am Jesus whom thou persecutest...

So we can see that Hutter's Hebrew made no distinction between Jehovah and Jesus in his Hebrew New Testament, fitting in with our Jehovah/Jesus study earlier. In Hutter's Dodecaglott, the Tridaic Declaration can be related to either Jesus or the Father, as clearly both are Jehovah.

Also of note, in Hutter's Dodecaglott the Greek ἐρχόμενος is in Revelation 16:5 as pictured below:

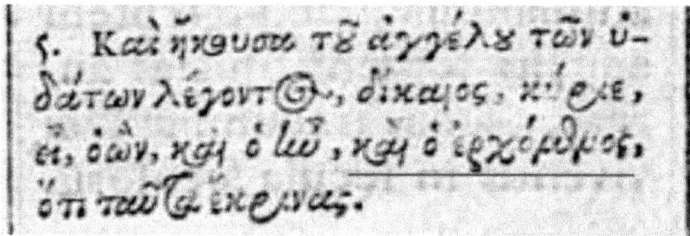

Revelation 16:5 in Hutter's 1599 Greek has καὶ ὁ ἐρχόμενος

Notice also that Hutter has **ἐρχόμενος** while Beza has **ἐσόμενος**. Hutter's ἐρχόμενος translates as "is to come" while ἐσόμενος means "shalt be", or "will be".

Καὶ ἤκουσα τοῦ ἀγγέλου τῶν ὑδάτων λέγοντος, δίκαιος, κύριε, εἶ ὁ ὢν καὶ ὁ ἦν καὶ **ὁ ἐρχόμενος**, ὅτι ταῦτα ἔκρινας·[84] - Hutter

So we can see that Hebrew expert Hutter followed the conclusions in the annotations of Erasmus for his Greek, and the same conclusions of Beza in the Hebrew. Aside from his Hebrew having "shalt be", the French also has

---

[84] (Novum Testamentum Domini: nostri: Iesu. Christi. Syriacè, Ebraicè, Graecè, Latinè, Germanicè, Bohemicè, Italicè, Hispanicè, Gallicè, Anglicè, Danicè, Polonicè. 2 vols. Edited by Elias Hutter and Jacob Coler.)

"qui seras" (shalt be) instead of "qui est à venir" (is to come). We can clearly see the link from "I AM", "Jehovah", to "shalt be", in the Hebrew, which is read "is to come" in his reference in the Greek.

2.4 Commentaries Concerning the Triadic Declaration

With the above in mind, let's look at how commentaries in Revelation 1:4 link the Triadic Declaration to both Jehovah and the I AM. I have emphasized the relevant parts via bold and underline. I hope the commentaries below are not tedious to the scholar as they are provided for the average Christian to shw common evidence of the link between Jehovah, I AM, and the Triadic Declaration. Many of these examples simply speak for themselves. Later, we shall examine what Beza said in Revelation 1:4 and how the footnote in his 1598 Annotations clearly point to this verse to explain Revelation 16:5, something White never mentions.

Adam Clarke in his Commentary says concerning Revelation 1:4:

> From him which is, and which was, and which is to come - This phraseology **is purely Jewish**, and probably taken from the **Tetragrammaton, יהוה Yehovah**; which is supposed to include in itself all time, past, present, **and future.** But they often use the phrase of which the ὁ ὤν, καὶ ὁ ἦν, καὶ ὁ ἐρχόμενος, of the apostle, is a literal translation.
> So, in Sohar Chadash, fol. 7, 1: "Rabbi Jose said, By the name Tetragrammaton, (i.e. יהוה, Yehovah), the higher and lower regions, the heavens, the earth, and all they contain, were perfected; and they are all before him reputed as nothing; יהיה והוא הוה היה והוא יהוא והוא vehu hayah, vehu hoveh, vehu yihyeh ; and He Was, and He Is, **and He Will Be**.

So, in Shemoth Rabba, sec. 3, fol. 105, 2: "The holy blessed God said to Moses, tell them: - לבוא לעתיד הוא ואני עכשיו הוא ואני שהייתי אני ani shehayithi, veani hu achshaiu, veani hu laathid labo ; I Was, I Now Am, and **I Will Be in Future**." In Chasad Shimuel, Rab.

Samuel ben David asks: "Why are we commanded to use three hours of prayer? Answer: These hours point out the holy blessed God; ויהיה הוה היה שהוא shehu hayah, hoveh, veyihyeh ; he who Was, who Is, and **who Shall Be**. The Morning prayer points out him who Was before the foundation of the world; the Noonday prayer points out him who Is; and the Evening prayer points out him **who Is to Come**."

This phraseology is exceedingly appropriate, and strongly expresses the eternity of God; for we have no other idea of time than as past, or now existing, or **yet to exist**; nor have we any idea of eternity but as that duration called by some aeternitas a parte ante, the eternity that was before time, andaeternitas a parte post, the endless duration that **shall be** when time is no more. That which Was, is the eternity before time; that which Is, is time itself; and **that which Is to Come**, is the eternity which **shall be** when time is no more.[85]

Ellicott's in his Commentary for English Readers at Revelation 1:4 related the I AM to the Triadic Declaration:

From him which is, and which was, and **which is to come** (or, **which cometh**).—The phrase presents a remarkable violation of grammar; but the violation is clearly intentional. It is not the blunder of an illiterate writer; it is the deliberate putting in emphatic form the **"Name of Names."** "Should not," says Professor Lightfoot, "this remarkable feature be preserved in an English Bible? If in **Exodus 3:14** the words run, '**I AM**

---

[85] Clarke, Adam. "Commentary on Revelation 1:4". "The Adam Clarke Commentary". //m.studylight.org/commentaries/acc/revelation-1.html. 1832.

hath sent me unto you,' may we not also be allowed to read here, from 'HE THAT IS, AND THAT WAS, AND THAT **IS TO COME**?'" The expression must not be separated from what follows. The greeting is triple: from Him which is, and which was, and which cometh; from the seven Spirits; and from Jesus Christ—**i.e., from the Triune God.** The first phrase would therefore seem to designate God the Father, the self-existing, eternal One, the fount and origin of all existence. Professor Plumptre suggests that the phrase used here may be used in allusion and contrast to the inscription spoken of by Plutarch, on the Temple of Isis, at Sais: "I am all that has come into being, and that which is, **and that which shall be**; and no man hath lifted my vail." The heathen inscription identifies God with the universe, making Him, not an ever-being, but an ever-becoming, from whom personality is excluded: the Christian description is of the personal, everlasting, self-revealing God—who is, who was, **and who cometh**. We should have expected after "is" and "was" "**will be**;" but there is no "**will be**" with an eternal God. With Him all is; so the word "**cometh**" is used, hinting His constant manifestations in history, and the final coming in judgment. This allusion to the Second Coming is denied by Professor Plumptre, but as he admits that the words, "**He that cometh**," used in the Gospels, and applied by the Jews to the Messiah, may be designedly employed here by the Apostle, it is difficult to see how the Advent idea can be excluded. The word appears to imply that we are to be always looking for Him whose "**comings**" recur in all history as the earnests of the fuller and final Advent.[86]

In the 1910 The Expositor's Greek Testament in Revelation 1:4, many of the concepts above are discovered:

---

[86] Ellicott, Charles John. "Commentary on Revelation 1:4". "Ellicott's Commentary for English Readers". "//m.studylight.org/commentaries/ebc/revelation-1.html. 1905.

ἀπὸ ὁ ὤν, κ. τ. λ., a quaint and deliberate violation of grammar (Win. § 10, IC.; Moult, Revelation 1:9) in order to preserve the immutability and absoluteness of the divine name from declension, though it falls under the rule that in N.T. and LXX parenthetic and accessory clauses tend to assume an independent construction. The divine title is a paraphrase probably suggested by rabbinic language (e.g., Targum Jonath. apud Deuteronomy 32:39, ego ille, qui est et qui fuit **et qui erit**); the idea would be quite familiar to Hellenic readers from similar expressions, e.g., in the song of doves at Dodona (ζεὺς ἦν, ζεὺς ἔστιν, **ζεὺς ἔσσεται**) or in the titles of Asclepius and Athene.

Simon Magus is said to have designated himself also as ὁ ἑστὼς, ὁ στὰς, ὁ στησόμενος, and the shrine of Minerva (= Isis) at Sais bore the inscription, I am all that hath been and is and shall be: my veil no mortal yet hath raised (Plut. de Iside, 9), the latter part eclipsed by the comforting Christian assurance here. ἦν, another deliberate anomaly (finite verb for participle) due to dogmatic reasons; no past participle of εἰμί existed, and γενόμενος was obviously misleading. **ὁ ἐρχ**., instead of **ὁ ἐσόμενος**, to correspond with the keynote of the book, struck loudly in Revelation 1:7. In and with his messiah, Jesus, God himself comes; **ἐρχ**. (the present) acquires, partly through the meaning of the verb, **a future significance**.[87]

In the 2013 Expository Notes of Dr. Thomas Constable on Revelation 1:4, he correctly mentions Revelation 16:5 and Exodus 3:14 as being part of the group of Triadic Declarations:

> John sent this letter (the whole book) to the seven churches mentioned in chapters 2, 3, which Since this book deals mainly with future events, John described the

---

[87] Nicol, W. Robertson, M.A., L.L.D. "Commentary on Revelation 1:4". The Expositor's Greek Testament. "//m.studylight.org/commentaries/egt/revelation-1.html". 1897-1910.

divine Author as God (the Father) who Isaiah, was, and **is to come**. This title occurs nowhere else in the Bible except in Revelation (Revelation 1:8; Revelation 4:8; cf. Revelation 11:17; **Revelation 16:5**; Exodus 3:14-15). This description stresses the continuity of God's sovereign dealings with humankind.[88]

Albert Barnes' Notes on the Whole Bible:

From him which is, and which was, and which is to come - From him who is everlasting - embracing all duration, past, present, **and to come**. No expression could more strikingly denote eternity than this. He now exists; he has existed in the past; **he will exist in the future**.....

He goes on:

Such a word would not be inappropriately paraphrased by the phrase "who is, and who was, and **who is to come**," or **who is to be**; and there can be no doubt that John referred to him here as being himself the eternal and uncreated existence, and as the great and original fountain of all being.

It is remarkable that there are some passages in pagan inscriptions and writings which bear a very strong resemblance to the language used here by John respecting God. Thus, Plutarch (De Isa. et Osir., p. 354.), speaking of a temple of Isis, at Sais, in Egypt, says, "It bore this inscription - ‹I am all that was, and is, and **shall be**, and my vail no mortal can remove'" - Ἐγώ εἰμι πᾶν τὸ γεγονός, καὶ ὄν, **καὶ ἐσόμενον** καὶ τὸν ἐμὸν πέπλον οὐδείς τω θνητὸς ἀνεκάλυψεν Egō eimi pan to gegonoskai hon **kai esomenon** kai ton emon peplon oudeis tō thnētos anekalupsen So Orpheus (in Auctor.

[88] Constable, Thomas. DD. "Commentary on Revelation 1:4". "Expository Notes of Dr. Thomas Constable". "//m.studylight.org/commentaries/dcc/revelation-1.html". 2012.

Lib. de Mudo), "Jupiter is the head, Jupiter is the middle, and all things are made by Jupiter." So in Pausanias (Phocic. 12), "Jupiter was; Jupiter is; Jupiter **shall be**." The reference in the phrase before us is to God as such, or to God considered as the Father.[89]

John Gill's Exposition of the Whole Bible at Revelation 1:4 speaks about the etymology of Jehovah here:

> **from him which is, and which was, and which is to come**; which some understand of the whole Trinity; the Father by him "which is", being the I am that I am; the Son by him "which was", which was with God the Father, and was God; and the Spirit by him "**which is to come**", who was promised to come from the Father and the Son, as a Comforter, and the Spirit of truth: others think Christ is here only intended, as he is in Revelation 1:8 by the same expressions; and is he "which is", since before Abraham he was the "I am"; and he "which was", the eternal Logos or Word; and "**is to come**", as the Judge of quick and dead. But rather this is to be understood of the first Person, of God the Father; and the phrases are expressive both of his eternity, he being God **from everlasting to everlasting**; and of his immutability, he being now what he always was, and **will be** what he now is, and ever was, without any variableness, or shadow of turning: they are a periphrasis, and an explanation of the word "**Jehovah**", which includes all tenses, past, present, **and to come**. So the Jews explain this name in Exodus 3:14,
>
> "Says R. Isaac, the holy blessed God said to Moses, Say unto them, I am he that was, and I am he that now is, and **I am he that is to come**, wherefore אהיה is written three times.

---

[89] Barnes, Albert. "Commentary on Revelation 1:4". "Barnes' Notes on the New Testament". "//m.studylight.org/commentaries/bnb/revelation-1.html. 1870.It

And such a periphrasis of God is frequent in their writings,[90]

Theodore Beza himself wrote the notes in the 1599 Geneva Bible at Revelation 1:4 & 1:8 which says:

> b. Revelation 1:4 That is, from God the Father, **eternal, immortal, immutable**: whose **unchangeableness** S. John declareth by a form of speech which is undeclined. For there is no incongruity in this place, where, of necessity the words must be attempted unto the mysteries, not the mysteries corrupted or impaired by the word....

> c. Revelation 1:4 By these three times, Is, Was and **shall be**, is signified this word **Jehovah**, which is the proper name of God....

> k. Revelation 1:8 A confirmation of the salutation aforegoing, taken from the words of God himself: in which he avoucheth his operation in every single creature, the immutable **eternity that is in himself**, and his omnipotence in all things: and concludeth in the unity of his own essence, that Trinity of persons, which was before spoken of....

> l. Revelation 1:8 I am he before whom there is nothing, yea, by whom everything that is made, was made **and shall remain** though all they should perish....[91]

---

[90] The New John Gill's Exposition of the Entire Bible Modernised and adapted for the computer by Larry Pierce of Online Bible. All Rightes Reserved, Larry Pierce, Winterbourne, Ontario. A printed copy of this work can be ordered from: The Baptist Standard Bearer, 1 Iron Oaks Dr, Paris, AR, 72855 Gill, John. "Commentary on Revelation 1:4". "The New John Gill Exposition of the Entire Bible". "//m.studylight.org/commentaries/geb/revelation-1.html". 1999.
[91] Beza, Theodore. "Commentary on Revelation 1:4". "The 1599 Geneva Study Bible". "//m.studylight.org/commentaries/gsb/revelation-1.html". 1599-1645.

Commentary Critical and Explanatory on the Whole Bible at Revelation 4:1 it should naturally read "He that shall be":

> **him which is ... was ... is to come** — a periphrasis for the incommunicable name Jehovah, the self-existing One, unchangeable. In *Greek* the indeclinability of the designation here implies His unchangeableness. Perhaps the reason why "He **which is to come**" is used, instead of "**He that shall be**," is because the grand theme of Revelation is the Lord's *coming* (Revelation 1:7). [92]

Robertson's Word Pictures in the New Testament at Revelation 1:4 links Exodus 3:14 to the Triadic Declaration, and reveals that the same triadic idiom is in Revelation 16:5.

> **From him which is** (απο ο ων — *apo ho ōn*). This use of the articular nominative participle of ειμι — *eimi* after απο — *apo* instead of the ablative is not due to ignorance or a mere slip (λαπσυς πενναε — *lapsus pennae*), for in the next line we have the regular idiom with απο των επτα πνευματων — *apo tōn hepta pneumatōn* It is evidently on purpose to call attention to the eternity and unchangeableness of God. Used of God in **Exodus 3:14**.

> **And which was** (και ο ην — *kai ho ēn*). Here again there is a deliberate change from the articular participle to the relative use of ο — *ho* (used in place of ος — *hos* to preserve identity of form in the three instances like Ionic relative and since no aorist participle of ειμι — *eimi* existed). The oracle in Pausanias X. 12 has it: ευς ην ευς εστι ευς εσσεται — *Zeus ēno ερχομενος* — *Zeus*

---

[92] Jamieson, Robert, D.D.; Fausset, A. R.; Brown, David. "Commentary on Revelation 1:4". "Commentary Critical and Explanatory on the Whole Bible". "//m.studylight.org/commentaries/jfb/revelation-1.html". 1871-8.

estio εσομενος — *Zeus essetai* (Zeus was, Zeus is, Zeus **will be**).

Which is to come (*ο ερχομενος* — *ho erchomenos*). "**The Coming One**," futuristic use of the present participle instead of *απο των επτα πνευματων* — *ho esomenos* See the same idiom in Revelation 1:8; Revelation 4:8 and (without *των* — *ho erchomenos*) in Revelation 11:17; **Revelation 16:5**. [93]

Vincent's Word Studies at Revelation 1:4 shows that the Triadic Declaration is a paraphrase of Exodus 3:14 and compares it to Revelation 16:5. He recognizes that the purest form of the Triadic Declaration is ὁ ἐσόμενος, *which shall be*, which was also the conclusion of Beza:

From Him which is, and which was, and which is to come (ἀπὸ τοῦ ὁ ὢν καὶ ὁ ἦν καὶ ὁ ἐρχόμενος)

The whole salutation is given in the name of the Holy Trinity: the Father (Him which is, and was, and **is to come**), the Spirit (the seven spirits), the Son (Jesus Christ).....This portion of the salutation has no parallel in Paul, and is distinctively characteristic of the author of Revelation. It is one of the solecisms in grammatical construction which distinguishes this book from the other writings of John. The Greek student will note that the pronoun *which* (ὁ) is not construed with the preposition *from* (ἀπό), which would require the genitive case, but stands **in the nominative case**.

Each of these three appellations is treated as a proper name. The Father is *Him which is, and which was, and which is to come*. This is a paraphrase of the unspeakable name of God (Exodus 3:14), the absolute and unchangeable. Ὁ ὢν, *the One who is*, is the Septuagint translation of Exodus 3:14, "I am the ὁ ὢν (*I am*):" " ὁ ὢν (*I am*), hath sent me unto you." *The One who was* (ὁ ἦν). The Greek has no imperfect participle, so that the finite verb is used. *Which is* and *which was* form one clause, to be balanced against **which is to come**. Compare Revelation 11:17; **Revelation 16:5**; and "was (ἦν) in the beginning with God" (John 1:2). *Which is to come* (ὁ ἐρχόμενος). Lit., *the **One who is coming**.* This is not equivalent to **who shall be**; i.e., the author is not intending to describe the abstract existence of God as covering the future no less than the past and the present. If this had been his meaning, he would have written **ὁ ἐσόμενος , which shall be**. The phrase **which is to come** would not express the **future eternity** of the Divine Being. The dominant conception in the title is rather that of *immutability*. Further, the name does not emphasize so much God's abstract existence, as it does His permanent covenant relation to His people. Hence the phrase **which is to come**, is to be explained in accordance with the key-note of the book, which **is the second coming of the Son** (Revelation 1:7; Revelation 22:20).

The phrase **which is to come**, is often applied to the Son (see on 1 John 3:5), and so throughout this book. Here it is predicated of the Father, apart from whom the Son does nothing. "The Son is never alone, even as Redeemer" (Milligan). Compare "**We will come** unto him," John 14:23. Origen quotes our passage with the words: "But that you may perceive that the omnipotence of the Father and of the Son is one and the same, hear John speaking after this manner in Revelation, 'Who is, etc.'" Dean Plumptre compares the inscription over the temple of Isis at Sais in Egypt: "I am all that has come

84

into being, and that which is, **and that which shall be**, and no man hath lifted my veil." [94]

Wesley in his Explanatory Notes at Revelation 1:4 says of Jehovah:

> From him who is, and who was, and **who cometh**, or, **who is to come** - A wonderful translation of the great name **JEHOVAH**: he was of old, he is now, **he cometh**; that is, **will be for ever**. [95]

Johann Albrecht Bengel's Gnomon of the New Testament at Revelation 1:4 says:

> ἀπὸ ὁ) *Erasmus* introduced ἀπὸ τοῦ ὁ.**(5)** This is the first of those passages in which the reviewer says, that I cannot at all be defended. And yet the reading approved of by me, ἀπὸ ὁ, is an early one. See App. Crit. Ed. ii. on the passage: *When I pray, will they be moved, who, in their ignorance, esteem the press of Stephens of more value than all the traces of John in Patmos?—* ἀπὸ ὁ ὢν καὶ ὁ ἦν **καὶ ὁ ἐρχόμενος**, *from Him, who is, and who was,* **and who cometh**) In this salutation, James Rhenferd, in his Dissertation respecting the cabalistic **(6)** style of the Apocalypse, seeks for a description of the Ten Sephiroth, **(7)** three superior, and seven inferior: and he has proved that there is some resemblance; but he has brought forward from the Cabalistic writers nothing which does not exist in a purer form in the writings of John. Comp. Lamp. Comm. on the Apoc., p. 253.

---

[94] Vincent, Marvin R. DD. "Commentary on Revelation 1:4". "Vincent's Word Studies in the New Testament". "//m.studylight.org/commentaries/vnt/revelation-1.html". Charles Schribner's Sons. New York, USA. 1887.
[95] Wesley, John. "Commentary on Revelation 1:4". "John Wesley's Explanatory Notes on the Whole Bible". "//m.studylight.org/commentaries/wen/revelation-1.html". 1765.

The Hebrew noun יהוה is undeclined; and of that noun this is a periphrasis, ὁῶν καὶ ὁ ἦν **καὶ ὁ ἐρχόμενος**, as we shall see presently at Revelation 1:8. And therefore the periphrasis also is used without inflexion of case. The article ὁ, three times expressed, gives to the Greek paraphrase of a Hebrew noun the form of a noun. [96]

Matthew Poole in his English Annotations on the Holy Bible at Revelation 1:4 relates both the I AM and Jehovah to the Triadic Declaration, as was common in the reformation period:

> **From him which is, and which was, and which is to come:** these words are a description of God, particularly of Jesus Christ in his eternity and immutability: he was from eternity; he is now; and **he shall be for ever**. Or, (as some), he was in his promises before his incarnation; he is now God manifested in the flesh; and he is to come as a Judge, to judge the quick and the dead. This was an ancient name of God, Exodus 3:14, *I am that I am.—I AM hath sent me unto you.* These words interpret the name *Jehovah*.[97]

Justin Edwards wrote in his Family Bible New Testament concerning Revelation 1:4:

> **Which is, and which was, and which is to come**; that is, the self-existent and eternal God, who has life in himself. The words seem to be an exposition of the meaning of the Hebrew word Jehovah. [98]

---

[96] Bengel, Johann Albrecht. "Commentary on Revelation 1:4". Johann Albrecht Bengel's Gnomon of the New Testament.
"//m.studylight.org/commentaries/jab/revelation-1.html. 1897.
[97] Poole, Matthew, "Commentary on Revelation 1:4". Matthew Poole's English Annotations on the Holy Bible. "//m.studylight.org/commentaries/mpc/revelation-1.html". 1685.
[98] Edwards, Justin. "Commentary on Revelation 1:4". "Family Bible New Testament". "//m.studylight.org/commentaries/fam/revelation-1.html". American Tract Society. 1851.

In the *Cambridge Greek Testament for Schools and Colleges* at Revelation 1:4 it relates the I AM and Jehovah to the Triadic Declaration:

> ὁ ὤν καὶ ὁ ἦν καὶ ὁ ἐρχόμενος. A paraphrase of the "Ineffable name" revealed to Moses (Exodus 3:14 sq.), which we, after Jewish usage, write "Jehovah" and pronounce "the LORD." Or, rather perhaps, a paraphrase of the explanation of the Name given to him l. c., **"I am That I am"**—which is rendered by the LXX. Ἐγώ εἰμι ὁ ὤν, by the Targum of Palestine on Exod. "I am He who is, and **who will be."** The same Targum on Deuteronomy 32:39 has "Behold now, I am He who Am and Was **and Will Be.**" Probably ὁ ἐστὼς, ὁ στάς, ὁ στησόμενος, the Title which according to the ἐγάγη Ἀπόφασις Simon blasphemously assumed to himself, was the paraphrase of the same Name current among Samaritan Hellenists. [99]

Whedon in his *Commentary on the Bible* at Revelation 1:4 says:

> **was... to come**—The threefold divisions under which our minds are obliged to think all time, and so used to express the eternity of **Him**. The **threefold phrase** expresses the import of the word **JEHOVAH**. The elevation of the prophetic style induces the seer to refer to this name for God; and from the reverence with which the utterance of the divine name was avoided by the Jews, he gives the import, and not the name itself. The phrase, though dependent on the preposition form, is **sacredly preserved by John as a *nominative*,** thus

---

[99] "Commentary on Revelation 1:4". "Cambridge Greek Testament for Schools and Colleges". "//m.studylight.org/commentaries/cgt/revelation-1.html". 1896.

attaining an expressive emphasis above the ordinary rules of grammar.[100]

So as we can see from the varied commentaries above, the information Beza had about the Triadic Declaration was not some strange revelation, but a common theme flowing throughout history. There is an endless list of Scholars who relate the Triadic Declaration to Jehovah and I AM. Later we shall read the statements of Beza in his annotations and these commentaries at the first mention of the Triadic Declaration in Revelation 1:4 will be of importance also in answering White's false claims.

2.5 Similar Triadic verses and concepts

We see many triadic patterns in scripture:

> the Father, the Word, and the Holy Ghost
> the Father, and of the Son, and of the Holy Ghost:
> yesterday and today and forever.
> which is, and which was, and which is to come
> which is, and which was, and which is to come
> which was, and is, and is to come
> which art, and wast, and art to come
> which art, and wast, and shalt be

Imagine if it said in Hebrews 13:8 'Jesus Christ the same, yesterday and today and holy.' It would make no sense and a logical enquiry into it would ensue. The normal logical flow is, yesterday, and today, and forever. This verse, even though it has no others specifically like it, shows a basic pattern of past, present, and future. Even just with *one* verse, the

---

[100] "Commentary on Revelation 1:4". "Cambridge Greek Testament for Schools and Colleges". "//m.studylight.org/commentaries/cgt/revelation-1.html". 1896.

internal evidence cries out for a complete reading. Of how much more does Revelation 16:5, with all of the internal evidence involved, and as we shall see, external evidence, to not evaluate this verse would only be due to a bias against it. These type of triadic patterns are all though scripture. For example, there are eight triadic passages referring to Peter James and John:

Now the names of the twelve apostles are these: The first, Simon, who is called **Peter**, and Andrew his brother; and **James** the son of Zebedee, **and John** his brother; - Matthew 10:2

And after six days Jesus taketh **Peter, James, and John** his brother, and bringeth them up into an high mountain apart, Matthew 17:1

And he suffered no man to follow him, save **Peter, and James, and John** the brother of James.- Mark 5:37

And after six days Jesus taketh *with him* **Peter, and James, and John**, and leadeth them up into an high mountain apart by themselves: and he was transfigured before them. Mark 9:2

And as he sat upon the mount of Olives over against the temple, **Peter and James and John** and Andrew asked him privately, Mark 13:3

And he taketh with him **Peter and James and John**, and began to be sore amazed, and to be very heavy; Mark 14:33

And when he came into the house, he suffered no man to go in, save **Peter, and James, and John**, and the father and the mother of the maiden. Luke 8:51

And it came to pass about an eight days after these sayings, he took **Peter and John and James**, and went up into a mountain to pray. Luke 9:28

This random example reveals to us patterns in biblical grammar. John M. Frame wrote an interesting section in his book *The Doctrine of God* called *A Fascinating Look At 112 Triads Illuminating the Trinity*. On his blog he summarizes the Appendix, which is worth a look considering the subject at hand. He also makes some notes on the points. [101] It must be noted that there are very important twofold distinctions in Scripture such as the Old and New Covenants, Creator and created, as well as fourfold, sevenfold, tenfold, etc. But the triadic threefold distinctions are pervasive in scripture, and they hold special interest for our present discussion on Revelation 16:5.

Triads in scripture are very common, and we could write another article about Trinitarian triads, but I will leave that to your personal study. Many concepts also illuminate the Trinity, such as yolk, white, and shell; liquid, solid, and gas; height, width, and length; root, trunk, and branches; thought, word, and deed; husband, wife, and child; I, IV, and V, the three primary chords; defined by triads of tones; root position and two inversions of triadic chords; melody, harmony, and rhythm; observable concepts such as the three grammatical persons: I, you, and he; grammar, rhetoric, and dialectic—the classic trivium; red, yellow, and blue the primary colors; also concepts of the Trinity etc.

There are many others dealing directly with spiritual truth such as prophet, priest, king; revelation, inspiration, and illumination; omnipotence, omniscience,

---

101   https://verticallivingministries.com/2012/04/04/a-fascinating-look-at-112-triads-illuminating-the-trinity-by-john-m-frame/

and omnipresence; miracles as signs, wonders, and powers; creation of heaven, earth, and sea; the sun, moon, and stars; the three parts of the Old Testament in the Hebrew Bible: the Law, the Prophets, and the Writings; also triads in bible stories and laws such as: three stories in Noah's ark; three sending's of birds after the Flood; three sons of Noah; three visitors to Abraham; three patriarchs; three divisions of the tabernacle; three feast periods; three offerings; cleansing of a leper by blood, water, and oil on the ear, thumb, and toe (Leviticus 14:1-20); three years in Jesus' ministry; Jesus' parable of the talents (Matt. 25:14-30) describes three stewards: one increased the Lord's investment, then a second did, but the third did not; His three temptations; three prayers at Gethsemane; the three crosses; three days in the grave; concepts of faith, hope, and love 1 Corinthians 13:13; the three lusts in 1 John 2:16; great commandments: love God, love yourself, and love your neighbor; the world, the flesh, and the devil, the list is endless...

While this is one of the reasons for an investigation into the Triadic Declaration becoming a mere dyadic declaration in Revelation 16:5 in many modern versions, it is only a small part. White claimed:

> "Theodore Beza, for example, in Revelation 16:5 looked at the Greek text and all the Greek texts say the same thing, but he didn't like the way it went. And so he changed the word "holy" to the future form of the verb "to be," sort of, to make it nice and poetic and rhythmic. [102]

---

[102] (*The King James Controversy Revisited – 2002*, on the Ankerberg show, with Dr. Kenneth Barker, Dr. Don Wilkins, Dr. Daniel B. Wallace, Dr. James White, Dr. Samuel Gipp, Dr. Thomas Strouse, Dr. Joseph Chambers.)

But that is certainly not the only reason. White did not mention the Triadic Declaration and its etymological link to Jehovah, or I AM, nor the fact that the entire phrase is nominative (a name), nor did he mention other documents which contain "shalt be" as we shall see. At the beginning of this chapter I quoted the union/onion Wallace comment, certainly not because I think the individual words *esomenos* and *osios* sound the same as White claims was Beza's reasoning. White makes two assertions with the above statement, firstly that Beza thought ἐσόμενος became corrupted into ὅσιος because of similarities between the lettering, and then adds that it was done to harmonize with the other four Triadic Declarations.

> "...Theodore Beza, for example, in Revelation 16:5 looked at the Greek text and all the Greek texts say the same thing, but he didn't like the way it went. And so he changed the word "holy" to the future form of the verb "to be," sort of, to make it nice and poetic and rhythmic "

White is either ignorant, and his scholarship on this issue is deeply flawed, or he is being deliberately deceptive about the reasons Beza did what he did. I will give him the benefit of the doubt and say White is ignorant on this issue. I mean just look at his book. He provides a picture in his book which he proudly promoted on the Dividing Line as the go-to manual on this issue, but the photo of Coverdale does not even have the actual quote of Revelation 16:5 in the entire picture, either in English or Latin. The verse cuts out at the bottom.

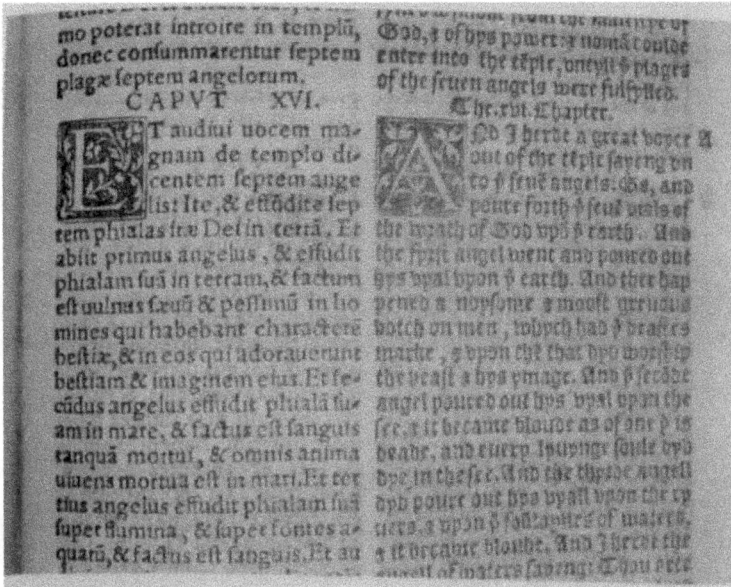

The picture in White's book The King James Only Controversy shows Coverdale entirely without the actual Revelation 16:5 quote. It seems White also mistook the Latin Sanguis for Sanctus.

How White originally made this blunder, has not seen it in its final draft, and how this error still exists since 2009 with no one picking up on that error is beyond me. But it reveals his level of scholarship and shows how many people have actually examined or critiqued what he claims. He also says that another picture is the Stephanus edition of 1555 when in fact it is the 1550 edition. He also keeps saying that the reading was not seen before 1598, but it was in Beza's 1582, 1588, and 1594 Annotations. White compounds his ignorance with such error and it is usually topped off with his own pride. Honest and decent bible believers are labeled deceivers by him. He is not trustworthy.

2.6 Nomina Sacra

Nomina sacra was used widely and early in biblical manuscripts. The reverence for God and eventually other divine concepts, would have been used in the Jehovic Triadic Declaration of Revelation 16:5. In some early Greek and Latin New Testament printed editions, the nomina sacra is kept in many verses, but Stephanus and later Beza unwrapped most of these in the latter editions of the New Testament to make the full reading of the text more readable and understandable in Greek and Latin.

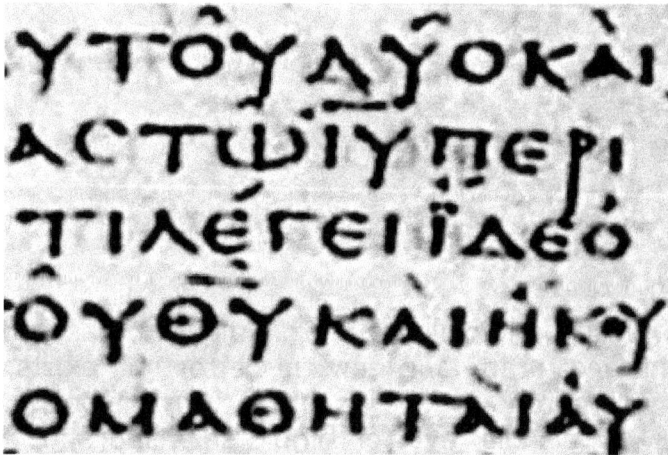

Two *nomina sacra* are highlighted, IY and ΘY, representing *Jesus* and *God* respectively, in this passage from John 1 in Codex Vaticanus (B), assumed to be from the 4th century but not yet scientifically validated.

Since we have established that the New Testament translations of "I AM" and "Jehovah" are distinctly relative to "which art, wast, and shalt be", which has its own distinct Strong's Concordance Dictionary reference number, being *the* most holy name in scripture, *the* Sacred Name, and being *the* purest form of the five Triadic Declaration's in Revelation, it makes perfect and logical sense to acknowledge that early scribes wrote "holy" in Greek "hosios", or Latin "Sanctus", to designate the Triadic Declaration in Revelation 16:5 as a *nomin sacrum.* Nomina sacra (singular: nomen sacrum) is Latin for "sacred name", and is the scribal practice of abbreviating or replacing divine names or titles, especially in Greek, but it also occurs in some form in Latin, Coptic, Armenian, Gothic, Old Nubian, and Cyrillic. The usual abbreviated nomen sacrum form consists of two or more letters from the original word spanned by an overline. Metzger lists 15 such expressions from Greek papyri: the Greek counterparts of *God, Lord, Jesus, Christ, Son, Spirit, David, Cross, Mother, Father, Israel, Savior, Man, Jerusalem,* and *Heaven.* * The KJV Today website points out some unusual nomina sacra:

> In P75 at John 3:8, both the noun, "πνεῦμα" (wind) and the verb, "πνεῖ" (blows) are written as nomina sacra. This peculiar nomen sacrum at John 3:8 was not carried over in future manuscripts. However, it goes to show that just about anything that is remotely divine qualified as a nomen sacrum.[103]

It is thought that the initial system of nomina sacra consisted of just four or five words, called *nomina divina*: the Greek words for *Jesus, Christ, Lord, God,* and possibly *Spirit*. The practice quickly expanded to a number of other words regarded as sacred. In the system of nomina sacra that came to prevail, abbreviation is by *contraction*, meaning that the first and last letter (at least) of each word are used. But in a few early cases, an alternate practice is seen of abbreviation by *suspension*, meaning that the initial two letters (at least) of the word are used; e.g., the opening verses of Revelation in Papyrus 18 write Ἰησοῦς

---

[103] http://www.kjvtoday.com/home/translation-issues/shalt-be-or-holy-one-in-revelation-165

Χριστός (*Jesus Christ*) as IH XP. Contraction, however, offered the practical advantage of indicating the case of the abbreviated noun. Although I would disagree with the regular concept of an entire BC Greek LXX as many believe, it is common knowledge that the Hebrew Tetragrammaton appears in early Greek Old Testament editions. The New International Dictionary of New Testament Theology (1984, Volume 2, page 512) says:

> "Recent textual discoveries cast doubt on the idea that the compilers of the LXX [Septuagint] translated the tetragrammaton YHWH by kyrios. The oldest LXX MSS (fragments) now available to us have the tetragrammaton written in Heb[rew] characters in the G[ree]k text. This custom was retained by later Jewish translators of the O[ld] T[estament] in the first centuries A.D."

In the James White - Jack Moorman debate of 2011, White claimed that nomina sacra was developed because the early Christians "would actually use abbreviations to try to get more onto a page." But it is far more feasible that it began as an adaptation of the custom in Hebrew writing of lettering the name of God with special inscription. In early Greek Old Testament copies, kurios was substituted for the sacred tetragrammaton and was given special treatment to distinguish it from the occurrences in which it did not refer to God. This reveals White's illiteracy on the issue of nomina sacra, and even a cursory look at the manuscripts involved reveal that nomina sacra lettering are sometimes large, and also the margins in many of the early manuscripts have an abundance of space. The fact that White is illiterate concerning such nomina sacra and its development, shows that from the initial stages of this argument the ignorance is only compounded. White is ignorant of the Triadic Declaration, of it being the Name of Jehovah/I AM, of how nomina sacra developed from the tetragrammaton, and of how these details are explained in Beza's footnotes in Revelation 16:5 and 1:4.

The use of nomina sacra was an act of sacred reverence rather than a purely practical space-saving device. It arose from the Jewish practice of writing the divine name as the Hebrew tetragrammaton in early Greek Scriptures and abbreviating such proper names. There is a distinction between abbreviated nomina sacra and the nomina sacra concerning the Tetragrammaton. Using the first and last letter and contracting names may have been inspired by Jesus, as He speaks of himself as "the beginning and the end" and "the first and the last" as well "the Alpha and the Omega". The very concept of the name of James White's ministry is a nomen sacrum description of Jesus, the Alpha and Omega. What a pity he knows so little about the practice. You only have to listen to White's drivel concerning the greatest grammatical error in the critical Greek text at 1 Timothy 3:16 to see the compounding errors of White concerning nomina sacra, where he assumes the reading of "hos" over a well established abbreviated form of "Theos", causing a predicate to not have a subject, thus giving rise to the blizzard and completely false assumption that the verse was an ancient hymn. Even the NKJV has the verse in strophes (making it look like a hymn or poem) following such nonsense. White ruins the verse, as text critics so often do. It is clearly nomina sacra form, not OC (who).

Most instances of nomina sacra are an abbreviation, not a substitution or replacement of one word for another, *except* in the case for the Tetragrammaton. Over the centuries, various translators have inserted the Tetragrammaton into Hebrew versions of the New Testament. One of the earliest Rabbinical translations of Matthew is mixed in with the 1385 critical commentary of Shem-Tob, in which he includes the Tetragrammaton written out or abbreviated 19 times, while occasionally including the appellative *HaShem* (השם, meaning "The Name").

Many modern Jews pen "L-rd" or "G-d", as many erroneously believe that the vowels of Elohim and Adonai were inserted onto the tetragrammaton to avoid mentioning the Sacred Name. It is a very common Jewish exercise to restrict the use of the sacred names of God to a liturgical context. In casual conversation some Jews, even when not speaking Hebrew, will call God *HaShem* (השם), which is Hebrew for "the Name" (Leviticus 24:11; Deuteronomy 28:58). Likewise, when quoting from the Tanakh or prayers, some Jews even replace *Adonai* with *HaShem*. For example, when making audio recordings of prayer services, *HaShem* will generally be substituted for *Adonai*.

Historically, when this Jewish practice towards the Sacred Name was applied, the name must firstly be recognized by the expert scribe called a *sofer*, who writes such Torah scrolls. A psychological preparation is made before transcribing and once he begins a name he is not permitted to stop until it is finished, and he must not be interrupted while writing it, even to greet a king. If an error is made in writing it is not to be erased, but a line must be drawn around it to show that it is disregarded, then the entire page must be put in a *genizah*, which is a burial place for scripture, and a new page rewritten. This unusual practice is said to be from Deuteronomy 12:3–4 which reads:

> And ye shall overthrow their altars, and break their pillars, and burn their groves with fire; and ye shall hew down the graven images of their gods, and destroy the names of them out of that place. Ye shall not do so unto the Lord your God. - Deuteronomy 12:3–4

From this verse it is understood by some Jews that one should not erase or blot out the Sacred Name of God. However, other information reveals that if the name of God was written upon an unorthodox or heretical manuscript, then it should be burnt. While none of the extant Greek manuscripts of the New Testament contain the Tetragrammaton, except in its expanded form in the five Triadic Declarations, a passage recorded in the Hebrew Tosefta, Shabbat 13:5, quoting Tarfon is sometimes cited to suggest that early Christian writings or copies not only contained the Tetragrammaton but that they were to destroy such manuscripts entirely:

> The Gilyon[im] (i.e., gospel books) and the books of the minim (i.e., Jewish heretics) are not saved [on the Sabbath] from fire; but one lets them burn together with the names of God written upon them. – Shabbat 13:5[104]

In the 1st and 2nd Century, Rabbi Jose the Galilean, said:

> "one cuts out the references to the Divine Name which are in them [the Christian writings] and stores them away, and the rest burns." *

It is interesting that in the *Anchor Bible Dictionary*, Howard states:

> There is some evidence that the Tetragrammaton..... appeared in some or all of the OT quotations in the NT when the NT documents were first penned.

In the book *Archaeology and the New Testament*, John McRay wrote of the possibility that the New

---

[104] The **Jewish Encyclopedia** (1910) defines the word *Gilyonim* in the **Talmud** as referring to the **Gospels** in the time of **Tarfon**. see **Ludwig Blau**, 1910 JewishEncyclopedia.com - GILYONIM

Testament autographs may have retained the divine name in quotations from the Old Testament[105] In 1871 Robert Baker Girdlestone, concerning the Tetragrammaton, stated that if the Septuagint had used:

> "one Greek word for Jehovah and another for Adonai, such usage would doubtless have been retained in the discourses and arguments of the N.T. Thus our Lord in quoting the 110th Psalm,...might have said 'Jehovah said unto Adoni.'"[106]

Since Girdlestone's time it has been shown that the Septuagint (so called) contained the Tetragrammaton, but that it was removed in later editions.[107] Wolfgang Feneberg comments in the Jesuit magazine *Entschluss / Offen* (April 1985):

> Ile [Jesus] did not withhold his father's name YHWH from us, but he entrusted us with it. It is otherwise inexplicable why the first petition of the Lord's Prayer should read: 'May your name be sanctified!'"

Feneberg further notes that

> "in pre-Christian manuscripts for Greek-speaking Jews, God's name was not paraphrased with kýrios [Lord], but was written in the tetragram form in Hebrew or archaic

[105] McCray, John, Archaeology and the New Testament Baker Academic (1 February 2008)ISBN 978-0801036088
[106] https://books.google.com.au/books?id=m51r0dP4MToC&pg=PA43&lpg=&redir esc=y#v=onepage&q&f=false
[107] The New International Dictionary of New Testament Theology (1984, Volume 2, page 512) says: "Recent textual discoveries cast doubt on the idea that the compilers of the LXX [Septuagint] translated the tetragrammaton YHWH by kyrios. The oldest LXX MSS (fragments) now available to us have the tetragrammaton written in Heb[rew] characters in the G[ree]k text. This custom was retained by later Jewish translators of the O[ld] T[estament] in the first centuries A.D."

Hebrew characters... We find recollections of the name in the writings of the Church Fathers".

Nomina sacra with the supralinear stroke, which is an indicator used in Greek writing to designate letters being read as numbers, came out of a desire for the word ιησους, or rather the abbreviation IH, to be read as the number 18 because it would correspond to the Hebrew ח which is pronounced "Hi", meaning life. This is documented as "gematria", which is the practice of reading a religious meaning into the numerical values of letters in Holy texts and is generally associated with "ancient Jewish exegesis" (Hurtado, 114).[108] Thus, ancient Greek letters with a line above them were to be recognized as numbers. A modern example of an infamous name contraction concerns Adolf Hitler, of whom Neo-Nazis use the number 88 as an abbreviation for the Nazi salute Heil Hitler. The letter H is eighth in the alphabet, whereby 88 becomes HH.

In the Latin, the Tetragrammaton is abbreviated in the form of "dns" or "dni" with a long line above the "n". The Greek fragment of the Book of Leviticus, manuscript 4Q120 displays the divine name in Greek characters, as ΙΑΩ, which has been called the *trigrammaton*, in Leviticus 3:12 (frg. 6) and 4:27 (frg. 20). The usual method of substituting the Tetragrammaton with κύριος ("Lord") was not practiced here. The Codex Marchalianus also uses the trigrammaton ΙΑΩ to transcribe the tetragrammaton.

---

[108] Larry Hurtado's *The Earliest Christian Artifacts: Manuscripts and Christian Origins.*

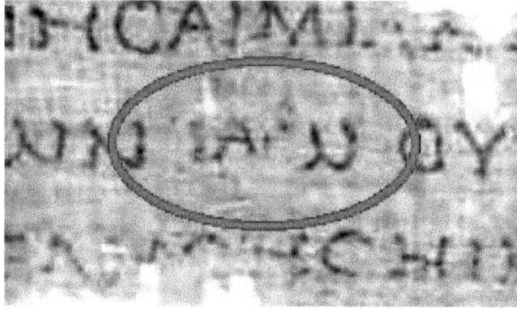

In 4Q120 and Codex Marchalianus the
trigrammaton IAΩ is used to transcribe the tetragrammaton.

This *sigla* IAΩ would later come to signify Jesus as a
sacred abbreviation in place of the Greek words *Iesous
Alpha Omega* Jesus Beginning and End.[109] Shortened
forms of the Tetragrammaton appear in several
languages. Beside the biblical names containing Jehovah
being shortened by scribes, such as described earlier
like "Jehosophat" into "Jesophat", many times in the Old
Testament versions Jehovah is completely transliterated
to the point where ancient lettering remains, with
examples of Latin DS, Dominus, Greek KC, Kurious, and
others.

There is evidence for Christian scribes endeavoring to
preserve the representation of the Tetragrammaton in
Hebrew square letters within copies of the Greek Old
Testament[110] other evidence [111] shows the Greek letters
PIPI being used in some contexts, indicating that
Christian scribes might attempt to preserve a form of
the Tetragrammaton in palaeo-Hebrew characters.[112] So
either with a Jewish scribe using nomina sacra or with a
Christian scribe attempting to reproduce the
Tetragrammaton in palaeo-Hebrew character, it reveals

---

[109] Cf. Epiphanius, ca. 380 CE.
[110] p. 303 - Mercati Hexapla (Rahlfs 1098)
[111] Marchalianus [Rahlfs 2125] and TS 12.182 [Ralhfs 2005]
[112] (p. 304).

another instance of the Sacred Name being transliterated.

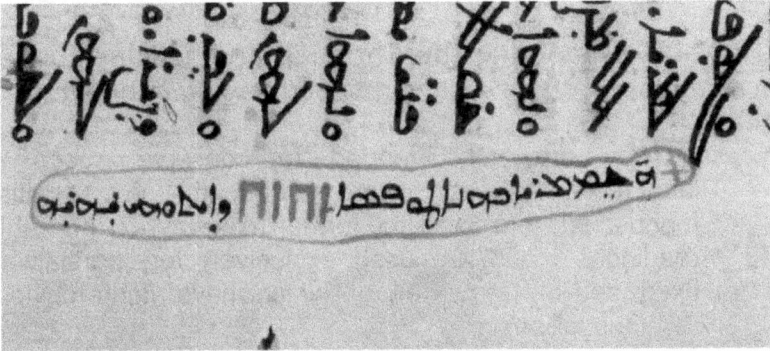

A Syriac Manuscript, MBM 1, f. 105v, with a (sideways) marginal note to Ex 28:37, containing the Greek letter form of the Hebrew tetragrammaton in red.[113]

P967 (LXX 4) contains Greek and Hebrew nomina sacra in the same document. There is also the embedding of the tetragrammaton in paleo-Hebrew lettering in the Greek manuscripts P.Oxy. 50.3522 and 8HevXIIgr. Emanuel Tov noteed that Qumran often replaces the Name with "four or five dots, sometimes preceded by a colon",[114] and P.Oxy. 7.1007 and P967 both bear the replacement of the tetragrammaton with two paleo-Hebrew *yods*. The two yods which bear the vowel points for Adonai is still a common method for presenting the Covenant Name in liturgical works today, nearly two thousand years later. Kurt Treu in his *Die Bedeutung des Griechischen für die Juden in vömischen Reich* said of contracting the translations of the *Tetragrammaton*:

> "[The phenomenon] began among Jews prior to Christian usage and initially included both *theos* and *kurios*, written as contractions with a

---

horizontal stroke placed over them to distinguish them in Greek texts where they served as translation equivalents of יהוה."

Hurtado, comparing the Christian and secular nomina sacra exposes White's flawed space saving concept:

> "They are not intended to conserve space or labor. They appear more frequently in Christian manuscripts prepared for formal usage, such as public readings... [and are used exclusively for] a relatively fixed set of terms, all of which have fairly obvious religious meaning."

It is also noteworthy that the indicator of a *nomin sacrum* is different than how abbreviations are indicated in common or secular texts. The supralinear stroke does not usually occur in non-religious literature except concerning numerals. Hurtado observes the reverence which is illustrated through the use of these sacred alternatives to fully spelling out divine names and titles.

> "In the nomina sacra, we encounter a fascinating manifestation of ancient Christian devotion."

Some ancient witnesses testify to manuscripts which used gold ink to letter the tetragrammaton, revealing the value people placed upon the Name.[115] Some forms in which the Tetragrammaton was written from a French site [116] include (excuse the French):

Désignation	Date	Formes du nom

---

[115] Josephus, *Antiquities* 12.89; *Aristeas* 176
[116] https://areopage.net/files/6.htm

		divin
<u>8HevXXIIgr</u>	I (fin)	𐤉𐤄𐤅𐤄 𐤉𐤄𐤅𐤄
LXXIEJ 12	I (fin)	𐤉𐤄𐤅𐤄
<u>AqTaylor</u>	V - VI	𐤉𐤄𐤅𐤄
<u>AqBurkitt</u>	V-VI	𐤉𐤄𐤅𐤄
<u>SimP. Vindob.</u> <u>G.39777</u>	III - IV	𐤉𐤄 𐤉𐤄 𐤉𐤄𐤅𐤄
<u>Papyrus Fouad Inv.</u> <u>266</u>	-I	יהוה
Ambrosienne O 39 sup	IX (fin)	ΠΙΠΙ
<u>4QLXXLevb</u>	-I(fin) - I	ΙΑѠ
<u>LXX P. Oxy. VII.</u> <u>1007</u>	III	ZZ
LXX P. Oxy. 3522	I	ZЧZЄ
Sepher ben Sira (Siracide ou Ecclésiastique)	-III	,,,

La période intermédiaire (175 - 200 AD)
Cf. Robert Kraft : *Ambiguous Representations of the Tetragrammaton in Greek*.

Désignation	Date	Formes du nom divin
P. Oxy. 656 Bodleian Library MS. Gr. Bib. D.5 (P)	II	
P. Oxy. 1075	III	
P. Berlin 17213	III	

The above is just a small example of the Sacred Name in Old Testament literature. Unfortunately, many times the Jehovah's Witnesses have collected the most data on this issue, and google search will often yield J.W. material.

Others such as Greek author Pavlos D. Vasileiadis have given us some helpful insights into Greek literature and the Sacred Name. In his 2014 research article, *Aspects of rendering the sacred Tetragrammaton in Greek*, he explains the transmission of the Name in Greek and also explains its abbreviated and contracted forms.[117] What is most helpful in his article is the Appendix A where he lists the many different ways the Sacred Name has been rendered into Greek over time. Here is a sample of one of the lists he provides. The

---

[117] https://www.degruyter.com/downloadpdf/j/opth.2014.1.issue-1/
opth-2014-0006/opth-2014-0006.pdf

106

following few pics are placed here to emphasize my point about nomina sacra but I encourage you to research this fascinating material for yourself:

02. Possible Greek transcriptions of יהוה using vowels and consonants

Form	Pronunciation	Date	Reference
*Ιαχβά	/i.ax.'va/	–	
*Ιαχωβά / Ιαχωβᾶ / *Ιαχοβά	/i.a.xo.'va/	1883	Ιαχωβᾶ: Ιγν. Μοσχάκης [Ign. Moschakes], Μελέται και Λόγοι Εκκλησιαστικοί, 1883, p. 249.
*Ιαχωβάχ / *Ιαχοβόχ	/i.a.xo.'vax/	–	
Ιαχωβάς / *Ιαχοβάς	/i.a.xo.'vas/	1998	Graecised form. Ιαχωβάς: Λεξικό της κοινής νεοελληνικής, Ινστιτούτο Νεοελληνικών Σπουδών, Aristotle University of Thessaloniki, 1998, «ιαχωβάς».
Γιαχωβά / Γιαχωβᾶ / *Γιαχοβά	/ja.xo.'va/	1969	Γιαχωβᾶ: Γ. Μαγκλής [G. Magles] (Greek transl.), N. Καζαντζάκης [N. Kazantzakis] (French original), Γόντα-Ράμπα, εκδ. Καζαντζάκη, 1969, p. 64. Γιαχωβᾶ: Νέα Εστία [Nea Estia], no. 93 (1973), p. 397.
Γιαχωβάς	/ja.xo.'vas/	2008	Graecised form. Λ. Χρηστίδης [L. Chrestides], Μόναλογκ, εκδ. Κασταvιώτη, 2008, p. 102.
*Γιαχουάχ	/ja.xu.'ax/	–	
*Γιαχωβάχ / Γιαχοβάχ	/ja.xo.'vax/	–	
*Γιαχουβά	/ja.xu.'va/	–	
*Γιαχουβάς	/ja.xu.'vas/	–	Graecised form.
*Γιαχουβάχ	/ja.xu.'vax/	–	
Ιώβαχος	/i.'o.va.xos/	1622	N. Fuller, Miscellaneorum sacrorum libri duo, quintus & sextus, 1622, p. 194.
Ιωβά / Ιουά / *Ιοβά	/i.o.'va/	1618	Ιωβά: J. Drusius, Tetragrammaton, sive de Nomine Dei proprio, quod Tetragrammaton vocant, 1604, p. 106. Ιουά: N. Fuller, Miscellaneorum Theologicorum, quibus non modo scripturae divinae, 1618, pp. 189, 495.
*Ιώβε / *Ιόβε	/i.'o.ve/	–	Compare Lat. Iovis → Jove / dʒaʊv/ (Jupiter)
Ιεβέ	/i.e.'ve/	20th cent.	I. Καμπελής [I. Kampelis], «Ιαβέ», in the Νεώτερον Εγκυκλοπαιδικόν Λεξικόν (1948–1954), Vol. 9, p. 745. See also ιευέ above.
Ιάων	/i.'a.on/	4th cent. C.E.	Graecised form. PGM P XII 75.
*Ιάως / *Ιωάς	/i.'a.os/	–	Graecised form. Ιάως: Used in 1Ch 8:10, LXX (NETS: "Iaos") to translate the term יעוש

As one can see from just a cursory look, the full and contracted names with several variant forms appear. In Appendix B he offers several pictures concerning the Sacred Name including full names of Jehovah from the 13th century as Γεχαβά (Yehovah) below to lists of contracted forms (following page):

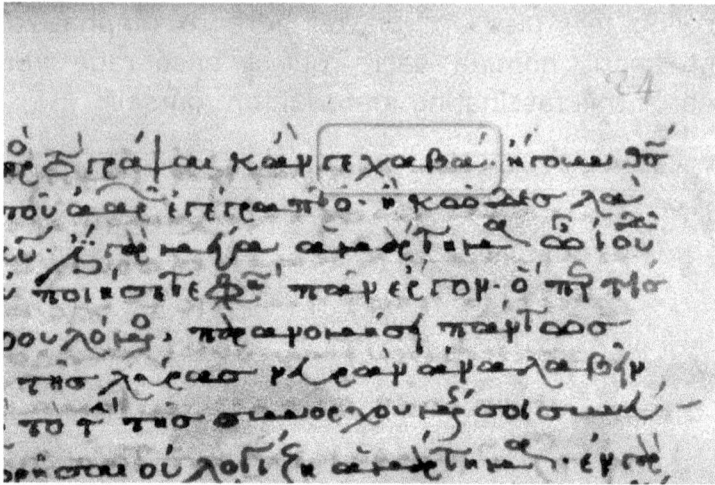

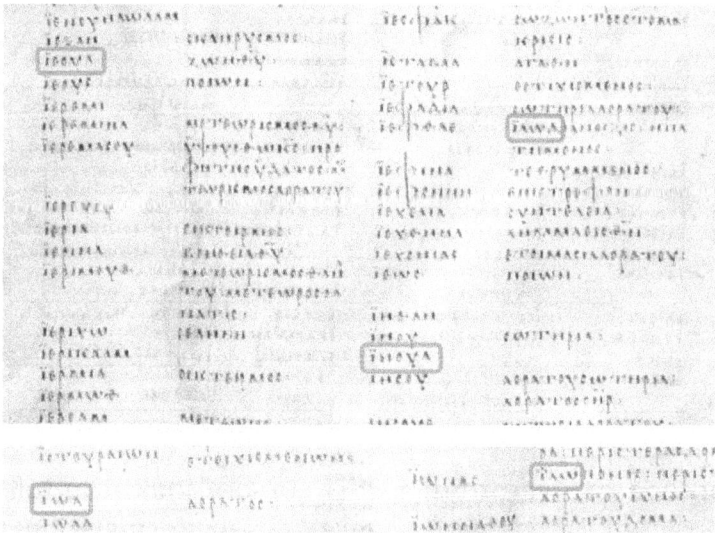

At times the nomina sacra was a simple symbol such as the staurogram (rho-cross) on this coin:

The staurogram ($\overset{p}{+}$, crossed P) is derived from the christogram $\ast$ and like the christogram is a monogram comprising the first two letters of Christ in Greek, Chi (X) and Rho (P). The staurogram symbol is also called a Rho-cross $\underset{\text{\&}}{\text{\&}}$. It is used as a control symbol on numerous late Roman coin issues. Justinian I issued a scarce nummus with the staurogram between alpha and omega as a "monogram" reverse type. In Song of Solomon the infamous Codex Sinaiticus does contain explicit references to the *dramatis personae* (Bride, Groom), and these could be considered sacred names, and they weren't contracted forms.

Why then would it seem strange that the purest formula of the Tetragrammaton in Revelation 16:5 would be unaffected by such trends. The "holy" is merely indicating the "sacred" as in *sacred* name. White is enraged at the removal of Holy in Rev 16:5 but also takes out 5 extra holies here in one of his favorite manuscripts:

> Revelation 4:8 "HOLY, HOLY, HOLY, Lord God Almighty, which was, and is, and is to come." (KJV)

But Sinaiticus says:

> Holy, holy, holy, holy, holy, holy, holy, holy, Lord God Almighty..."

So it is clear that certain scribes that I would reject, either as obviously corrupted, or as fraudulent,[118] but that White would esteem, were placing many extra holies into Revelation.

Again it is rather enlightening to appeal to a general bog standard like Wikipedia in the picture below, which summarizes this issue, much like the child pointing out that the king has no clothes on. Obviously this is a simplification of the issue at hand, but I was greatly amused when I saw it as it also corresponds with a reference which is interesting:

> "... The reference to God .... "the Holy One," "the Place," and "the Name." These appellations were by no means innovative ways of addressing God but they came up as part of a Jewish reverential nomenclature towards the end of the Second Temple period..." Page 58..."

Tetragrammaton

From Wikipedia, the free encyclopedia

For other uses, see Tetragrammaton (disambiguation).

"YHWH" redirects here. For the historic Iron Age deity, see Yahwen. For the modern Jewish conception of God, see God in Judaism and God religions.

The **tetragrammaton** (/ˌtɛtrəˈɡræmətɒn/; from Greek Τετραγράμματον, meaning "[consisting of] four letters"), יהוה in Hebrew and **YHWH** in Latin script, is the four-letter biblical name of the God of Israel.[1][2] The books of the Torah and the rest of the Hebrew Bible (with the exception of Esther and Song of Songs) contain this Hebrew name. Religiously observant Jews and those who follow Talmudic Jewish traditions do not pronounce יהוה, nor do they read aloud transliterated forms such as Yahweh; instead the word is substituted with a different term, whether used to address or to refer to the God of Israel. Common substitutions for Hebrew forms are *hakadosh baruch hu* ("The Holy One, Blessed Be He"), Adonai ("My Lord") or *HaShem* ("The Name").

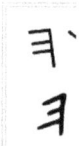

Amusingly the Tetragrammaton article on Wikipedia, it clearly summarizes this issue and says "Common substitutions ...are...The Holy One...".

---

[118] http://www.sinaiticus.net

2.7 Replacement of God's names

As we have seen, there has been a huge amount of effort by scribes in all cultures in the application of the tetragrammaton. There is an interesting way to understand such replacements by looking at a theological exercise in 1 Corinthians 13. Some preachers have suggested that because God is love, you could replace the word love (Charity) in 1 Corinthians 13 with the name Jesus. So the reading:

> **Charity** suffereth long, and is kind; **charity** envieth not; **charity** vaunteth not itself, is not puffed up, - 1 Corinthians 13:4

Would read:

> **Jesus** suffereth long, and is kind; **Jesus** envieth not; **Jesus** vaunteth not itself, is not puffed up,

Then to examine how much like Christ your actions are, you could replace it with your own name there:

> **Bob** suffereth long, and is kind; **Bob** envieth not; **Bob** vaunteth not itself, is not puffed up,

Instantly we are confronted with our areas of lack, and the perfect standard of Christ's love. A great exercise. But we could also do the same for many such names in scripture. Some exercises could include placing love in the place of the name Jesus, or truth, or many aspects of God's character. But likewise, with the information in this book, it would also be plausible to place "which art, wast, and shalt be" in the place of Jehovah or LORD in scripture, and also for Jesus. This would be an interesting exercise. "and Jesus (which art, wast, and shalt be) saith to him...". Even for those textual critics who reject the reading in Revelation 16:5 this exercise applies, because it is the name of God, the I AM & Jehovah.

2.8 Conjectural Emendations

James White said in The King James Only Controversy:

> So how does the AV defender respond to the documentation that the King James Version contains a reading created out of the mind of Theodore Beza, one unknown to the ancient church, unknown to all Christians until the end of the sixteenth century?[119]

Was this reading only in the mind of Beza? Was the reading unknown to *all* Christians until 1598 as White claims? Firstly, the definition of a conjectural emendation seems to range from having no Greek evidence, to having no evidence whatsoever. In his review of David Trobisch's article on the Nestle Aland 28 Edition, Dan Wallace makes specific reference to the definition of conjecture and why the NA 28 edition has eliminated references to them:

> Gone are any explicit conjectural emendations, whereas the NA27 listed over 100 of them (one of which was followed [Acts 16:12], though both Bruce Metzger and Kurt Aland disagreed with the rest of the committee), and NA28 adds one more to the text (2 Peter 3:10). (At the same time, neither of the variants in these two

119 White, James. The King James Only Controversy: Can You Trust the Modern Translations? (Updated June 1, 2009 Expanded edition), Minneapolis: Bethany House Publishers; Updated, Paperback: 368 pages, p. 237, ISBN-13: 978-0764206054

passages is a true conjecture since there are versions that have these readings. Bruce Metzger and Bart Ehrman, The Text of the New Testament, 4th ed. [Oxford: OUP, 2005] 230, implicitly define a conjecture as having no support in Greek manuscripts, versions, or fathers: the need for conjectural emendation for the New Testament is "reduced to the smallest dimensions" because "the amount of evidence for the text of the New Testament, whether derived from manuscripts, early versions, or patristic quotations, is so much greater than that available for any ancient classical author...")[120]

So according to White's senior tutors, Metzger and Ehrman, the strict definition of a conjectural emendation does not apply when a version or a quote from a father is found. So quotes containing "shalt be" have been found. This is why I said that White is off target, because beside the Ethiopic version, the Latin "futurus" of Beatus (referred to in Hoskier at Rev. 16:5 against what White says in his footnotes) equates to the Greek esomenos, and so this reading *does* have manuscript support within the closed class of Greek and Latin sources used for the Textus Receptus and we shall see more external evidence for esomenos in the next chapter. White is trying to claim that he has always meant that a conjectural emendation is when it is a Greek mss, but most other text critics differ with him. James White said in his book The King James Only Controversy:

> Beza did introduce... "conjectural emendations," that is, changes made to the text without any evidence from the manuscripts. A few of these changes made it into the KJV, the most famous being Revelation 16:5, "O Lord,

[120] https://danielbwallace.com/tag/conjectural-emendation

113

which art, and wast, and shalt be" rather than the actual reading, "who art and who wast, O Holy one."

But the NA 28 edition has several conjectural emendations that don't seem to worry James White who howls at those who defend the reading of "shalt be". But do any of the conjectural emendations in the modern Greek text have anywhere near the amount of validation as Revelation 16:5? For example, in Acts 16:12 and 2 Peter 3:10, why does White not howl at the scribes in Munster Germany like he does to those who defend the TR/KJV reading at Revelation 16:5? Jeff Riddle[121] reveals how at 2 Peter 3:10, in the NA 27 Edition, it was clearly marked as a conjecture, but in the NA 28 it is no longer marked. He also shared how White rebukes TR/KJV supporters for adopting 1 John 5:7, for not having the majority reading, but then White adopts readings with absolutely no evidence whatsoever and staunchly defends them! Anyone who reads White's response to Riddle will immediately see the double standards of White. Equitable Eclectic text proponent James Snapp Jr, who rejects the genuineness of the Johannine Comma picked up on the blatant inconstancy of White. Here is part of the article in which Snapp is quoted:

> Riddle's point was simple: if it is wrong to reject the Comma Johanneum on the grounds that its Greek support is relatively late and sparse, why is it right to accept the text in NA28 at Acts 16:12 and Second Peter 3:10, where the adopted reading has no Greek support at all? Whatever one thinks of the genuineness or non-genuineness of the CJ, Riddle's basic point is valid. White was in over his head, and it shows in his video.

---

[121] http://confessingbaptist.com/james-white-encouraging-christians-to-be-truthful-more-on-textual-criticism-slippery-slopes-more-dividing-line-audio-video/

And it does not salvage his case at all to divert viewers' attention to the Textus Receptus' reading in Revelation 16:5 (where the TR reading has no extant Greek support). Whether advocates of the Textus Receptus and/or KJV accept some conjectural emendations is not the question. The thing to see is that once one adopts any conjectural emendations in the New Testament text, one forfeits the right to use the "The Greek support for your favored reading is late and sparse" line as if it is absolutely decisive, because if it were /absolutely/ decisive, then the same principle would preclude the adoption of the NA28's readings in Acts 16:12 and at the end of Second Peter 3:10. Except it would carry even more force, inasmuch as the "late and sparse" Greek support for the CJ is still /something,/ whereas the Greek support for these two readings in the text of NA28 is non-existent.[122]

Although I believe Snapp is flawed in his Equitable Eclectic text position, with his rejection of the Comma Johanneum and other TR readings, I believe he is spot on in his evaluation of White here. Metzger admitted that the 24th edition of Nestle's Greek New Testament includes about 200 conjectures (p. 185), (mostly in footnotes). So it seems White and others have differing definitions concerning conjectural emendations.

White struggles with several verses concerning the deity of Jesus and the names of God. Besides thinking the slur Yah'weh is the name of God, several examples reveal to us that he is the pot calling the kettle black, or in other words, he performs the very practice of rejecting a well-established majority and adopting variants with little or even no manuscript evidence that he claims to be angry about. White advocates some very obscure readings with little or no evidence,

---

[122] http://www.jeffriddle.net/2014/09/word-magazine-27-rejoinder-james-white.html

including what he himself would consider conjectural emendations. Kenneth Sisam said that :

> "To support a bad manuscript reading is in no way more meritorious than to support a bad conjecture, and so far from being safer, it is more insidious as a source of error. For, in good practice, a conjecture is printed with some distinguishing mark which attracts doubt; but a bad manuscript reading, if it is defended, looks like solid ground for the defense of other readings." [123]

Beza conducted a meticulously close study of the text in its cultural and historical context which preceded with a thorough analysis of all extant versions and readings of the given fragment. He had intimate knowledge of writing style used by John. Holmes writes,

> "That there is considerably less need for emendation of the NT text than that of comparable documents is indeed true, but we must not confuse less need with no need."[124]

So most textual critics accept the need for conjecture, but White is only upset over what he labels as the conjecture in the TR/KJV text and not in the Critical Text.[125] But is this the reading of esomenos merely a conjecture? Let's look at the evidence concerning this,

---

[123] (Kenneth Sisam, "The Authority of Old English Poetical Manuscripts," now available in Studies in the History of Old English Literature, p. 39. This volume, despite its title, is largely devoted to textual questions, and much of the advice, including the above, is capable of application outside the context of Anglo-Saxon.)

[124] (Michael W. Holmes, "Reasoned Eclecticism in New Testament Textual Criticism," printed in Bart D. Ehrman & Michael W. Holmes, The Text of the New Testament in Contemporary Research, 1995, page 348. This section, pp. 346-349, is probably the best brief summary of the need for a more "classical" style of criticism.)

[125] It must be noted that James White did a Dividing Line program on Revelation 16:5 in which he seems to be making the new claim that any conjecture is wrong, shocking most listeners, as this goes against the NA28. This new development seems to have come about due to pressure from people like myself, Riddle, and Snapp, in pointing out such basic inconsistency. This occurred in 2019, whereas most of this chapter was relevant in 2016 when originally written.

which I think I have doubled, maybe tripled, in just one month looking at this issue for my original article, causing me to wonder what half of these textual scholars in Münster are doing with their time. Perhaps the Greek speaking church knew of this Nomen Sacrum but simply kept it as a scared name, like they did with many others?

While this book is being prepared for print, James White is often parroting information on his YouTube program from the book *Beyond What is Written* by Jan Krans. There is a glaringly inconsistent appeal from White to a book co-edited by Bart Ehrman, something he rebukes people of doing in his debates against Muslims, and also the strange affinity toward Krans who basically rejects and mocks the reconstructionist approach to recovering the "original autograph" as outdated. Krans is clearly at odds with White over exactly what a conjecture is. The following is from Jeff Riddle's Blog (emphasis mine):

> In the General Introduction between **two distinct types of emendations** which he suggests would have been used by scholars like Erasmus and Beza in their study of the text, and which JW might well have applied with profit to his study of the texts like Revelation 16:5.
>
> Krans says, "In this period, emendation, the adoption of alternative readings, was done in **two distinct ways**, depending on the way these readings were found: they could either be **derived from manuscripts** or be arrived at **by rational argument**. Hence a distinction was made between *emendatio codice ope* ('emendation by means of manuscripts') and *emendatio ingenii ope* ('emendation by means of reasoning')".[126]

---

[126] http://www.jeffriddle.net/2019/03/wm-120-white-krans-erasmus-and-beza-one.html

White has placed confusion upon these two issues by several errors: firstly not being in agreement with his peers as to the definition of a conjecture, as found in a *Greek* manuscript or as Metzger and Ehrman point out, *any* manuscript, and secondly conflating this issue with the conjecture of Beza which was derived from the rational argument of nomina sacra.

Revelation 16:5 is a unique passage in a unique book, concerning a unique name, describing the unique God. Whatever name people want to label Beza's reading is ok with me, as long as all of the appropriate information is given as to why Beza did what he did. Can the unwrapping of a nomen sacrum form of Jehovah be considered a conjecture, or just good scholarship? Those with a bias will disagree with Beza, but those with heart to understand will see a multifaceted issue, and not just a head count of manuscript readings containing "holy".

Carefully take note of the summery of the first two chapters: because early scribes wrote *sacred* or *osios* in the place of the expanded *name* of Jehovah and I AM, then this understanding should cause *all* Greek manuscripts to read as Beza's reading, just like how any other abbreviated name is expanded in scripture. Thus by adopting Beza's concepts here, all Greek manuscripts in fact point to esomenos. So the evidence for the reading in Greek manuscripts should now be counted as 100% instead of 0%.

CHAPTER 3

John did not write "and shalt be." He wrote "O Holy One." This is the united testimony of all relevant historical information. To deny this is to engage in the most egregious form of irrational thought. It is not *faith* to deny reality, it is *deception.* – James White, *The King James Only Controversy*[127]

3.1 EXTERNAL EVIDENCE AND PRE BEZA ALLUSIONS

Are TR/KJV defenders *deceived* as White claims? Are they *not in faith* and *irrational*? In this chapter we will look at the external evidence for the reading of "shalt be" in manuscripts, versions, church writers quotations, and early print editions until about the time of Calvin and Beza. The following chapter will look at the

---

[127] White, James. The King James Only Controversy: Can You Trust the Modern Translations? (Updated June 1, 2009 Expanded edition), Minneapolis: Bethany House Publishers; Updated, Paperback: 368 pages, p. 241, ISBN-13: 978-0764206054

timeframe beyond that. This chapter contains a basic chronological list of the evidence White refuses to look at and simply dismisses as irrelevant to our topic at hand.[128] White fails to enlighten his readers about all of the appropriate information.

Firstly, he fails to point out that only 4 manuscripts of Revelation 16:5 exist from before the 10th century and the 3 earliest Greek witnesses of Revelation 16:5 do not even agree!

The earliest witnesses to Revelation 16:5 read:

ο ων και ος ην και οσιος (Papyrus 47 3rd Century)
ο ων και ο ην ο οσιος (Sinaiticus fourth century)[129]
ο ων και ο ην οσιος (Alexandrinus fifth-century)

It seems the phrase got shorter with the passage of time. There is definitely not an agreement, as White claims in his book, since Alexandrinus has only οσιος. We can see from these three early witnesses that modifications set in early. "Lord" is also missing in some mss, yet is present in the Textus Receptus, although important, that is another topic entirely. "Holy" is reflected in modern versions, but none seem to follow the "and" of Papyrus 47.

---

[128] It must be acknowledged that some of the quotations allude directly to Revelation 16:5, others to I AM and Jehovah, and some to both. Due to the related nature of these instances, all are considered significant in this examination.
[129] Although this date has been hotly contested www.sinaiticus.net . It should be scientifically tested and dated.

3.2 P47

The infamous "και" of P47

The oldest Greek text of Revelation is P47, which is from the 3rd century, contains this passage, but it has a textual variant. It contains the "καὶ" (and) in Beza's phrase "καὶ ὁ ἐσόμενος". Modern textual scholars had rejected the καὶ of other manuscripts so prevalent in English bibles of the reformation such as the Geneva Bible with "and holy". But P47 was revealed in the 1930's. So they have reject the so called "oldest and best" reading of καὶ.

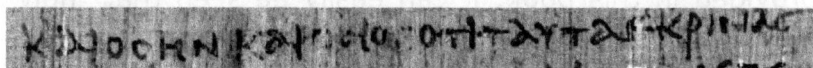

και ος ην και οσιος οτι ταυτα εκρινας (Papyrus 47) contains "και"

Several people have asked, "and..." what? What was P47 going on to read? Many reformation bibles, being more honest to the reading, had, "and holy" whereas White concludes the reading is indisputably "O Holy One" as if there are no variants. As we shall focus on soon, Beza has pointed out that in the manuscript for the Latin Vulgate for Revelation 16:5, the text was "*foolish and divisional*" because of the "and" but the same issue occurs here in P47, but modern textual critics reject the early papyrus reading of "καὶ" here as it caused the sentence to be *foolish and divisional*. James White feels that because those who defend the Ecclesiastical Text, or hold to a Textus Receptus position, can effortlessly provide a *mountain* of textual evidence to prove their Textus Receptus readings have a vast majority, that when on the rare occasion this is not the case, we are being inconsistent. But why then does the NA28 text reject the "καὶ" here? Why doesn't White follow the older Papyrus like he tells us to?

δίκαιος εἶ, ὁ ὢν καὶ ὁ ἦν, (*omitted καὶ*) ὁ ὅσιος, ὅτι ταῦτα ἔκρινας, [130]

The reading is clearly the Triadic Declaration but with (καὶ) ὁ ὅσιος which has been placed there to note nomen sacrum. Certain Critical Text advocates believe in a mythical *Lucianic Recension* in which almost all traces of a manuscript family can disappear, so why is it hard for them to concede that <u>one</u> word, which most certainly preserved as a rare nomen sacrum, became corrupted and misunderstood? But with the evidence provided in this book, it can easily be seen that "holy" relates to the purest form of nomina sacra regarding Jehovah and I AM, and not just the random reading of "holy". The methodology of modern textual critics is to follow the "oldest and best" manuscripts. But if they followed the "and" in P47 here they would end up with reading like this:

"Righteous art Thou, the Being One, and the One who was, **and** the Holy One."

James White in his book says:

---

[130] https://www.nestle-aland.com/en/read-na28-online/text/bibeltext/lesen/stelle/76/160001/169999/

Every Greek text-not just Alexandrian texts, but all Greek texts, Majority Text, the Byzantine text, every manuscript, the entire manuscript tradition-reads "O Holy One," containing the Greek phrase ὁ ὅσιος ("ho hosios").[131]

White is misleading here in omitting the information concerning the καὶ. He is making out that there is a consensus in the reading, but there is not. White has a habit of claiming conformity, when many times there are other variants to consider, such as in Revelation 15:3 where White attacks the TR reading but there are two other alternative readings. But he only attacks the TR reading leaving the other readings open for people to choose from.

3.3 Jerome has "shalt be"

Jerome (27 March 347 – 30 September 420) confirmed that there were a number of various Latin editions of the New Testament which differed in both translation and content before and around 405 AD (when Jerome finished his Vulgate). Most of these we do not have today. John Wordsworth (who edited and footnoted a three volume critical edition of the New Testament in Latin) revealed the like phrase in Revelation 1:4 "which is, and which was, and which is to come;" sometimes is rendered in Latin as "qui est et qui fuisti et futurus es" instead of the Vulgate "qui est et qui erat et qui uenturus est." (John Wordsworth, Novum Testamentum Latine, vol.3, 422 and 424.) Note that Wordsworth assumed that the quote was from Revelation 1:4, but it

---

[131] White, James. The King James Only Controversy: Can You Trust the Modern Translations? (Updated June 1, 2009 Expanded edition), Minneapolis: Bethany House Publishers; Updated, Paperback: 368 pages, p. 237, ISBN-13: 978-0764206054

reads just like Beatus whom we shall examine soon. Jerome said in *Sancti Eusebii Hieronymi epistulae*:

> sic et mille annorum spatia apud te, qui semper es **et futurus es** et fuisti...[132]

translated as

> so also the thousands of years of it to thee, **you shall be**, and you are, and have been...

Jerome has the exact reading of "shalt be". Again, White, and his crew would be cringing and I guess will have to demonize Jerome like they do Erasmus, Beza, and others. We can also see there have been different Latin translations of the verses involved. Primasius, Bishop of Hadrumetum, wrote a commentary on Revelation around 552 AD and used the Latin word "pius" instead of "sanctus."

Many manuscripts were destroyed, likely reflecting an inability of believers to renew and preserve true manuscripts due to widespread persecution & martyrdom in early centuries; persecution occurred in the 3rd century, under Roman emperor Decius, and destruction of scripture copies was a major goal of vicious empire-wide persecution in the early 4th century by Diocletian & Galerius, who sent out Roman soldiers to destroy all text copies; this persecution was concentrated in the eastern empire where the Traditional Text, the ancestor of the Textus Receptus, was the standard. But as we can see, White's assertion

---

[132] Title Sancti Eusebii Hieronymi epistulae: Epistulae CXXI-CLIV. Pars III, Page 2
Corpus scriptorum ecclesiasticorum latinorum, ISSN 1816-3882
Opere, Hieronymus (s.) S. Eusebii Hieronymi Opera, authored by Saint Jerome, Edited by Isidor Hilberg, Edition 2, Publisher   VÖAW, 1996, Original from   the University of Michigan, Digitized 1 Jul 2009, ISBN: 3700126026, 9783700126027, Length 515

is crumbling, and the list of people with the non nomina sacra reading here is mounting.

3.4 Clement of Alexandria

Clement of Alexandria (150 – 215) while writing about the Tetragrammaton, referred to God as "ο εσομενος" in The Stromata, Book V, 6:

> ἀτὰρ καὶ τὸ τετράγραμμον ὄνομα τὸ μυστικόν, ὃ περιέκειντο οἷς μόνοις τὸ ἄδυτον βάσιμον ἦν· λέγεται δὲ Ἰαού, ὃ μεθερμηνεύεται ὁ ὢν **καὶ ὁ ἐσόμενος.**

Translated as:

> Further, the mystic name of four letters which was affixed to those alone to whom the adytum was accessible, is called Jave, which is interpreted, "Who is **and shall be.**" [133]

With the revelation concerning the Triadic Declaration, the above reading has a remarkable resemblance with Beza's reading. Here is Beza's 1582, 1588, 1594, 1598 reading compared with Clements 3rd Century reading:

> ὁ ὢν, καὶ ὁ ἦν, καὶ ὁ ἐσόμενος – Beza 1582
> ὁ ὢν   καὶ ὁ ἐσόμενος – Clement 3rd Century

The Greek church writers used the future participle of ειμι to refer to the same Jehovah mentioned in Revelation 16:5. Clement said the interpretation of Jehovah has, "Who is and shall be." Was he speaking about how it is interpreted by

---

[133] (Christian Classics Ethereal Library)
http://ldysinger.stjohnsem.edu/@texts/0216_clement/04_myst_interp_tabern.htm

the apostle in the New Testament at Revelation 16:5? White will no doubt claim it is not related as he has already done here. If he knows he is cornered he will simply avoid the topic whatsoever. Look at what White says in his book:

> Thankfully, **there isn't the slightest doubt** as to what John wrote here, and **only misguided dedication to a human tradition would cause anyone to believe otherwise**. Christians are people of truth, and I truly exhort any KJV Only advocate to seriously consider this text, to examine the documentation provided, and to recognize King James Onlyism for what it is: **an unfounded tradition that flies in the face of the truth**.[134]

Clement related καὶ ὁ ἐσόμενος (shalt be) to Jehovah. I mean should I say case closed right there? This is the exact reading of Beza. But there is more to come.

3.5 Gregory of Nyssa

Gregory of Nyssa (335 – 395) referred to Christ as "ο εσομενος" in *On the Baptism of Christ*:

> Κοσμήτωρ δὲ πάντως τῆς νύμφης ὁ Χριστὸς **ὁ ὢν καὶ πρόων καὶ ἐσόμενος**, εὐλογητὸς νῦν καὶ εἰς τοὺς αἰῶνας τῶν αἰώνων, ἀμήν.

Translated as:

---

[134] White, James. The King James Only Controversy: Can You Trust the Modern Translations? (Updated June 1, 2009 Expanded edition), Minneapolis: Bethany House Publishers; Updated, Paperback: 368 pages, p. 241, ISBN-13: 978-0764206054

And verily the Adorner of the bride is Christ, **Who is, and was, and shall be**, blessed now and for evermore. Amen.[135]

Gregory of Nyssa clearly said Jesus is "who is, and was, **and shall be**". In the fourth century we have a Triadic Declaration, related to Jesus that has "and shall be". I thought James White said no one ever knew of the reading! White said:

Quite simply, before Beza, **no Christian had ever read the text the way the KJV has it today**.[136]

So White, although he has been shown several of these examples before, has simply shrugged them off, and claimed the reading has no evidence and those who think so are deceived.

3.6 Priscillian of Avila

Priscillian of Avila (340 – 385) wrote in Latin:

Ipse est enim qui fuit, est **et futurus est** et uisus a saeculis "verbum caro factus inhabitauit in nobis" (Jn 1:14)[137]

Translated as:

---

[135] Christian Classics Ethereal Library
http://www.ellopos.gr/mystics/gregory-of-nyssa/5.asp?pg=3

[136] White, James. The King James Only Controversy: Can You Trust the Modern Translations? (Updated June 1, 2009 Expanded edition), Minneapolis: Bethany House Publishers; Updated, Paperback: 368 pages, p. 241, ISBN-13: 978-0764206054

[137] Priscillian and Marco Conti. Priscillian of Avila: The Complete Works. Oxford: Oxford University Press, 2010. Print. Amazon [www.amazon.com/Priscillian-Avila-Complete-Oxford-Christian/dp/0199567379

He is that who was, is **and shall be**, and appeared as "the Word" from eternity, "was made flesh, dwelled in us," (Jn 1:14)

These are the same words Wordsworth mentioned concerning Vulgate readings.

3.7 Basil of Caesarea

Basil of Caesarea (The Great) in the 4th century has a reference to the Triadic Declaration in Eunomium Book 5 where he was expounding upon Hebrews 11:6 where Paul tells us to believe that God simply *is*:

μὴ γὰρ ὅ τι οὐκ ἔστιν. Ὁ γάρ ἐστιν, ἦν, καὶ ἔστι, καὶ ἔσται ἀεί· καὶ τοῖς πᾶσι τὸ εἶναι δωρεῖται, ὡς φύσει ὢν Θεός.

Translated as:

For what it "is," **it was, and it is, and it will always be**, and it gives the being [existence] to everyone, because it is He Who Is by nature.[138]

---

[138] In context:

Εἰ γὰρ αὐτῷ τῷ παναγίῳ Θεῷ τὰ περὶ αὐτοῦ ἀπιστοῦσι· πῶς τῶν προφητῶν αὐτοῦ ἢ ἀποστόλων ἀκούσωσι, λεγόν των ἐν θείαις Γραφαῖς τὰ περὶ αὐτοῦ καὶ τῶν εἰς αὐτὸν μελλόντων ἐλπίζειν; Πιστεῦσαι γὰρ δεῖ τὸν προσερχόμενον τῷ Θεῷ, ὅτι ἔστι. Πιστεῦσαι· μὴ γὰρ ἀπίστως περιεργάζεσθαι ὅ τί ἐστιν· μὴ γὰρ ὅ τι οὐκ ἔστιν. Ὁ γάρ ἐστιν, ἦν, καὶ ἔστι, καὶ ἔσται ἀεί· καὶ τοῖς πᾶσι τὸ εἶναι δωρεῖται, ὡς φύσει ὢν Θεός.

because if we refuse to to believe in the God three times holy himself, when he speaks of him, how could one then lend a docile ear to his prophets or his apostles, when, in the holy scriptures, they speak of Him or of those who owe hope in Him? "For he who comes to God must believe that He is" [Hebr., Xi, 6]. Pay attention to these words: they are as absolute as they are formal: it is necessary that the one who seeks God "believe that he is", and certainly not that he searches with an incredulous curiosity "what it is", for not to

The Latin in the text has:

Quod enim est, erat, et est, **et erit semper**

Translated as:

That is, was and is and **always will be**

The concept of Jehovah/I AM and the relative Triadic Declaration is unmistakably revealed here.

3.8 Epiphanius of Salamis

Epiphanius of Salamis (310 – 403) was bishop of Salamis, Cyprus, at the end of the 4th century. He was born in Palestine and spent a considerable part of his life there, gives Ἰά (Ia or Jah) and Ἰάβε (pronounced at that time /ja'vε/ most likely nomen sacrum for Yehovah) and explains Ἰάβε as meaning He who was and is and <u>always exists</u>.

...ὁ ὢν Κύριος Ἰάβε, ὅς ἦν καὶ ἔστι **καὶ ἀεὶ ὢν**.

Translated as:

---

say what it is not. **For what it "is," it was, and it is, and it will always be**, and it gives the being [existence] to everyone, because it is He Who Is by nature.

Translated by Charles Gordon Browne and James Edward Swallow. From Nicene and Post-Nicene Fathers, Second Series, Vol. 7. Edited by Philip Schaff and Henry Wace. (Buffalo, NY: Christian Literature Publishing Co., 1894.) Revised and edited for New Advent by Kevin Knight. >>www.newadvent.org/fathers/310241.htm

Migne Grace PG 29 751-752 PDF p. 70 - Migne Graeca PG 36, 441-442 [441B]

books.google.com/books?id=7fMUAAAAQAAJ&pg=PA411#v=onepage&q&f=false

…The LORD JEHOVAH He who was and is **and always exists.**[139]

3.9 Gregory of Nazianzus

Gregory of Nazianzus (329-390) in Oration 41 has:

ἦν μὲν ἀεὶ, καὶ ἔστι, **καὶ ἔσται**

Translated as:

> then, always existed, and exists, **and always will exist.**[140]

In context:

> The Holy Ghost, then, always existed, and exists, and always will exist. He neither had a beginning, nor will He have an end; but He was everlastingly ranged with and numbered with the Father and the Son.

This is clearly speaking of the eternality of the Holy Spirit. The Holy Ghost:

> then, always existed, (wast)
> and exists, (art)
> and always will exist. (shalt be)

---

[139] https://books.google.com.au/books?id=ixcRAAAAYAAJ&printsec=frontcover&source=gbs_ge_summary_r&cad=0#v=onepage&q&f=true) Epiphanius, Panarion, I, iii, 40, in P.G., XLI, col. 685

[140] Τὸ Πνεῦμα τὸ ἅγιον ἦν μὲν ἀεὶ, καὶ ἔστι, **καὶ ἔσται**, οὔτε ἀρξάμενον , οὔτε παυσόμενον, ἀλλ' ἀεὶ Πατρὶ καὶ Υἱῷ συντεταγμένον, καὶ συναριθμού μενον· οὐδὲ γὰρ ἔπρεπεν ἐλλείπειν ποτὲ, ἢ Υἱὸν Πα τρὶ, ἢ Πνεῦμα Υἱῷ.
The Holy Ghost, then, always existed, and exists, **and always will exist**. He neither had a beginning, nor will He have an end; but He was everlastingly ranged with and numbered with the Father and the Son.

3.10 Alcuin of York

Alcuin of York (735 – 19 May 804) was an English scholar, clergyman, poet and teacher from York, Northumbria. He was the student of Archbishop Ecgbert at York. At the invitation of Charlemagne, he became a leading scholar and teacher at the Carolingian court, where he remained a figure right up to the 790's. He wrote:

> Dominator Domine Deus omnipotens, qui es Trinitas una, Pater in Filio, Filius in Patre, cum Spiritu sancto: **qui es** semper in omnibus, **et eras** ante omnia, **et eris** super omnia Deus benedictus in saecula. [141]

Translated as:

> Sovereign Lord God almighty, who art Trinity together, the Father in the Son, the Son in the Father, with the holy Spirit: **who art** always in all things, **and wast** before all things, **and shalt be** God over all things blessed forever.

This represents the exact formula of Revelation 16:5:

> **who art** always in all things,
> **and wast** before all things,
> **and shalt be** God over all things blessed forever.

Because Alcuin of York wrote in the Latin we can compare it with Beza's 1582 Latin text which reads:

> Qui es, & Qui eras, & Qui eris,

---

[141] http://www.mlat.uzh.ch/MLS/xfromcc.php?tabelle=Alcuinus_cps2&rumpfid=Alcuinus_cps2,%20Officia%20per%20ferias,%20%20%20%20p87&id=Alcuinus_cps2,%20Officia%20per%20ferias,%20%20%20%20p87&level=3&corpus=2&current_title=

Alcuin:
> **qui es** semper in omnibus,
> **et eras** ante omnia,
> **et eris** super omnia Deus benedictus in saecula.

So here we have an English author with a reading strongly resembling that of Beza's Triadic Declaration about 700 years after John penned Revelation.

3.11 Beatus of Liébana

Spanish theologian Beatus of Liébana (730 – 800), wrote a popular commentary on the book of Revelation titled, *"Commentaria In Apocalypsin"*. The date of Beatus' readings may go as far back as 360 A. D. as Beautus relied on Tyconius' commentary on Revelation. It was hugely widespread in Europe and 31 manuscripts have survived. Considered together, the Beatus codices are among the most important Spanish medieval manuscripts and have been the subject of extensive scholarly and antiquarian enquiry.

472   S. BEATI IN APOCALYP.

INCIPIT TERTIUS ANGELUS.

Cap.XVI
v. 4.

"ET tertius Angelus effudit phialam suam in flumi-
na, & fontes aquarum, & factus est sanguis.
Et audivi vocem, Angelum aquarum dicentem : Justus es, qui fuisti, & futurus es Sanctus, quia hæc
judicasti : & quia sanguinem Sanctorum , & Prophe-
tarum effuderunt, sanguinem eis dedisti bibere : digni
sunt. Et audivi aram Dei dicentem : Etiam , Domine
Deus omnipotens : veræ & justæ sunt judicationes
tuæ." *Explicit.*

Beatus has "will be"
(Picture from KJV Today)

132

Beatus' excerpt of Revelation 16:5 has:

qui fuisti **et futures es**

Translated as:

which has been **and will be**

The context reads, "*Justus es, qui fuisti, & futurus es Sanctus*"[142] (*Just are you, which has been and will be the Holy One*). So it incorporates both readings, *and will be* and *the Holy One*. 31 existing manuscripts have the reading in Latin *& futurus es* which is the exact equivalent to καὶ ὁ ἐσόμενος, which is what Beza has in Revelation 16:5. With Beatus' book, there may have been several hundred copies that have been lost in time. For example, when the Complutensian Polyglot was printed, they ran 600 copies. Only 123 exist from that time (1514-1522). So we can see from that example that in just 500 years, a massive printed book like that can lose almost 80% of the copies. How much more so for older manuscripts. Depending on how you count variants, this would mean that the reading of "shalt be" appears here 62 times in 31 manuscripts. The fact that it appears in the main text as well as the commentary also speaks volumes. The fact that the commentary leans upon the 360 AD Tyconius' commentary also speaks volumes. Here is a latter English translation:

5 And I heard a voice from the waters say, Thou art righteous, O Thou, which wast, and shalt be holy, because thou hast judged thus.

---

[142] http://www.cehaq.fr/beatus/manuscrit/11.Beatus.Liber%20octavus.pdf

…and shalt be…[143]

The words in Latin *et futures es* or "shalt be"
appear twice in this picture at Revelation 16:5.

Above and below are pictures from one of the 31 editions.[144]

---

[143] English translation from:
(https://babel.hathitrust.org/cgi/pt?id=mdp.39015024256011;view=1up;seq=3)
[144] http://www.e-codices.unifr.ch/en/description/bge/lat0357
This is from the Genève, Bibliothèque de Genève, Ms. lat. 357 Parchment · 245 ff. · 25 x 16 cm · Italy / Southern Italy · 11th and 12th century. This manuscript was deposited in the Bibliothèque de Genève in 2007 by the priests of the Congregation of St. Francis de Sales (at the Institut Florimont in Geneva). This composite manuscript unifies two previously separate texts: a copy of Prician's Institutiones Grammaticae made during the 11th or 12th centuries in Italy, and the Commentary on the Apocalypse by Beatus of Liébana. The latter is illustrated with 65 miniatures; this 11th century copy was probably written in southern Italy, judging by the Beneventana and Carolingian minuscule scripts used.

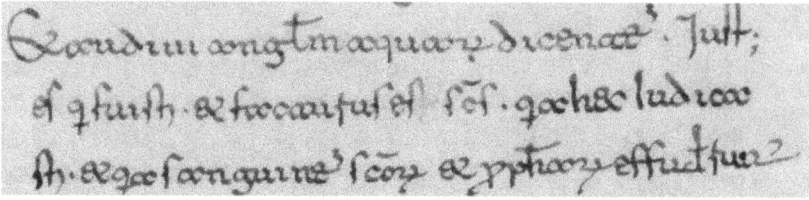

A close up of the verse in the main body of text

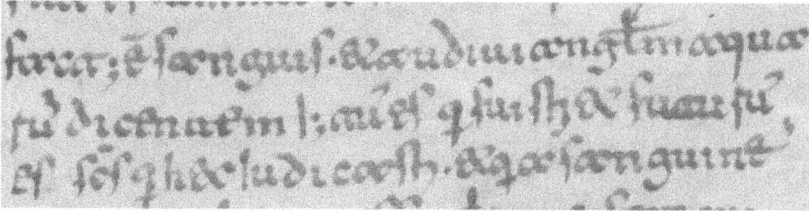

The verse in the commentary[145]

Beza most certainly knew of the Beatus reading, as the commentary it was a widely popular commentary. In the age of Beza, the Reformation Bible scholars were very deep readers of the early church writers. Beatus copied Old Latin versions as early as the fourth century which contained the reading esomenos. Beatus was making a compilation and thus preserving the work of Tyconius, who wrote his commentary on Revelation around 380 AD.[146] Besides this, the same reading was in Jerome.

3.12 Haimo Halberstadensis

Commentaria in Apocalypsin is a commentary on the book of Revelation written by 9th century German bishop Haimo Halberstadensis.[147]

---

[145] Images from http://www.e-codices.unifr.ch/en/description/bge/lat0357
[146] (Aland and Aland, 211 and 216. Altaner, 437. Wordsword, 533.).
[147]

http://books.google.ca/books?id=IM07AAAAcAAJ&printsec=frontcover&dq=commentaria

tę populi multi funt. [dicentem: luftus es qui eras fan
ctus.] Pręteritū tempus pofitum eft hic pro tribus tē
poribus, id eft, pro pręterito, pręfenti, & futuro. Qui
eras.f.iuftus es & eris.Quę iuftitia in hoc manifeftatur,
cum fubditur: [qui hęc]inquit[iudicafti, quia fanguinē

Picture and translation from KJV Today

The website KJV Today[148] says:

The text from "dicentem" to "eris" translated into English
is:

"[Saying: Thou art just, who were holy.] In past times it
is used here for three times, that is, for the past, present,
and future. Who were holy, are and shall be just."

There are two interesting features of this
commentary. First, the quotation from the biblical text,
[dicentem: Justus es qui eras sanctus.] is not Beza's
conjectured reading. However, it is neither the reading
found in the existing manuscripts nor in the Vulgate. The
reading, being translated, "You are just, who were holy"
is missing the clause, "and who are" (Latin: "& qui
es"). The Vulgate reads, "dicentem iustus es qui es et
qui eras sanctus".

Second, the commentary includes the sentence, "Who
were holy, are and shall be just", using the verbs, "eras",
"es" and "eris". The association of "justice" with the past,
present and future only occurs at Beza's Revelation
16:5. The previous triadic declarations at 1:4, 1:8, 4:8

+in+apocalypsin+haimo&source=bl&ots=cKguj5JI13&sig=9c1k8CKXsGcE4_7eSA3_dF1
tHFA&hl=en&ei=aTt4Td7qO8L7rAHShMDZCQ&sa=X&oi=book_result&ct=result&resnu
m=4&ved=0CC4Q6AEwAw
[148] https://sites.google.com/site/kjvtoday/home/translation-issues/shalt-be-or-holy-one-in-revelation-165

and 11:17 do not associate the formula with God's "justice". Haimo's commentary text carries the sense of Beza's Latin translation of his 1598 Greek Textus Receptus, which reads, "Justus es, Domine, Qui es, & Qui eras, & Qui eris". Beza chose "eris" as the Latin translation of "εσομενος" (shalt be), which is also the Latin word in Haimo's commentary. Haimo used "eris" (shalt be) for the future rather than "venturus est" (is to come) despite the previous occurrences of the formula in Revelation 1:4, 1:8 and 4:8 in the Vulgate having "venturus est" as the future.

It appears as though the original commentary included the biblical text as conjectured by Beza, and whoever compiled the present edition of the commentary took the commentary section from the original commentary and took the biblical text from a faulty version of the Vulgate.

This is another strong reference to the future aspect of the Triadic Declaration. But White again shrugs this off. But with the recent discovery of the Jerome quotation, it is perfectly plausible that the commentary was written concerning a reading Jerome had. This is something White mocked in his exposure of the "Yellow Post".[149]

3.13 Desiderius Erasmus

White claimed:

...there's not a question about it on anyone's part as to what that passage actually reads.[150]

---

[149] https://www.youtube.com/watch?v=dxCn5zA_DSo
[150] The King James Controversy Revisited - 2002
https://www.jashow.org/articles/general/the-king-james-controversy-revisited-program-3/
on the Ankerberg show, with Dr. Kenneth Barker, Dr. Don Wilkins, Dr. Daniel B. Wallace, Dr. James White, Dr. Samuel Gipp, Dr. Thomas Strouse, Dr. Joseph Chambers.)

So why then did Erasmus question it?

Q̄ui es,& qui eras.)Quanquam interpres mutauit perſonam,tamen to tidem ſyllabis dictū eſt,quibus ſuperius,Qui eſt,qui erat,qui uenturus eſt, ὁ ὢν,ὁ ἦν,ὁ ἐρχόμℓℴ⊙.

Erasmus at Revelation 16:5 in his annotations has ὁ ἐρχόμενος

In Erasmus' 1535 Annotations, he says:

> Qui es, & qui eras.) Quanquam interpres mutauit perfonam, tamen to tidem syllabis dictu est, quibus superius, qui est, qui erat, qui uenturus est, ὁ ὢν, ὁ ἦν <u>ὁ ἐρχόμενος</u>.

Translated as:

> Thou, who art, and who wast, the.) Although interpreter changed from, however to harmonize with the list mentioned above, who is, who was, who is to come, ὁ ὢν, ὁ ἦν <u>ὁ ἐρχόμενος</u>.

So if White had done a basic cursory check of the Annotations of Erasmus he would find the reading of "ὁ ἐρχόμενος". But this is not just in the latter editions of Erasmus, but in *all* five editions! See the 1516 below:

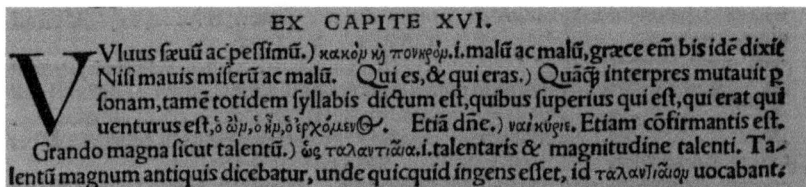

EX CAPITE XVI.

Vluus ſæuū ac peſſimū.) κακὸν κὴ πονηρὸμ.i.malū ac malū,græce em̄ bis idē dixit Niſi mauis miſerū ac malū. Qui es,& qui eras.) Quācþ interpres mutauit p fonam,tamē totidem ſyllabis dictum eſt,quibus ſuperius qui eſt,qui erat qui uenturus eſt,ὁ ὢμ,ὁ ἦμ,ὁ ἐρχόμεν⊙. Etiā dn̄e.) ναί κύριε. Etiam cōfirmantis eſt. Grando magna ſicut talentū.) ὡς ταλαντιᾶα.i.talentaris & magnitudine talenti. Ta- lentū magnum antiquis dicebatur,unde quicquid ingens eſſet, id ταλαντιᾶιομ uocabant.

Annotations on Revelation 16:5 Erasmus
shows reading ὁ ἐρχόμενος.[151]

---

[151] http://images.csntm.org/PublishedWorks/Erasmus_1516/Erasmus1516_0478b.jpg

In the dedication to Pope Leo X in his *Novum Instrumentum omne,* Erasmus said:

> "I have added annotations of my own, in order in the first place to show the reader what changes I have made, and why; second, **to disentangle and explain anything that may be complicated, ambiguous, or obscure.**"[152]

Erasmus included καὶ ὁ ὅσιος in his main text, but he clearly expressed doubt as to the authenticity of the reading in his annotations. The annotations are like a running commentary for the biblical text and reveal Erasmus' aims and methods. Erasmus was always striving for a faithful text that was understandable and correct to the Greek. Annotations revealed so much more than the one-sided meaning in the text. White bases his false claims upon half baked reading of the annotations of Beza, as we shall see soon, but then also failed to do rudimentary homework and look at Erasmus' work, which was passed over in silence and not mentioned once in White's book. It is not as if the reading was buried in a cave, even enemy of the Comma Johanneum Isaac Newton wrote in 1693 that Erasmus had ἐρχόμενος in his Annotations, and mentioned this basic fact in his notes on Revelation 16:5, 100's of years before White had access to Google search:

> καὶ ὁ ἦν, καὶ ὁ ὅσιος Erasm. \Syr. Primas/ **At in Notis Erasmus pro ὅσιος legit ἐρχόμενος**
> καὶ ὁ ἦν, **καὶ ὁ ἐσόμενος Bezæ codex antiquus**.

The underlined translates as:

---

[152] *Novum Instrumentum omne* http://www.e-rara.ch/bau_1/content/titleinfo/895554

"At the Notes Erasmus for ὅσιος read ἐρχόμενος"[153]

Newton left an observable paper trail for people like White to follow, but White knows very little about this topic and just claims Erasmus rejected the reading. In White's tirade against Luke Lubefore concerning the "Yellow Post" on this issue, White said:

> Why should I take Theodore Beza's conjectural emendation where he decides a reading on the basis of what he *likes*, and say that the mass of Christians believe this, when **nobody before Theodore Beza ever had the idea that Revelation 16:5 read that way**? Why should I believe that?"[154]

Note, the ignorance of the readings of Jerome, Clement, Beatus, Haimo, Erasmus, et al. Based on "what Beza likes"? I mean, who would not have read Erasmus' annotations, in *all* of his editions in the reformation? Um, *every* textual scholar would have. But, no, White claims "nobody before Theodore Beza ever had the idea that Revelation 16:5 read that way" or ever questioned the reading of "holy". How illiterate! But for those who know White's psuedoscholarship, it is not surprising.

3.14 Miles Coverdale

Miles Coverdale printed the first complete Bible containing the Old and New testaments in English in 1535. As mentioned earlier he has a very interesting

---

[153] ('Variantes Lectiones Apocalypticae' [version 1])
[154] The King James Controversy Revisited - 2002
https://www.jashow.org/articles/general/the-king-james-controversy-revisited-program-3/
on the Ankerberg show, with Dr. Kenneth Barker, Dr. Don Wilkins, Dr. Daniel B. Wallace, Dr. James White, Dr. Samuel Gipp, Dr. Thomas Strouse, Dr. Joseph Chambers.)

reading in Exodus 3:14, which corresponds to Luther's German reading:

> God saide vnto Moses: **I wyl be** what **I wyll be**. And he sayde: Thus shalt thou saye vnto ye children of Israel: **I wyl be** hath sent me vnto you. (Exodus 3:14)

Coverdale's "I wyll be" is the exact equivalent to Beza's "shalt be", except it is in the first person whereas "shalt be" is a second person declaration from the angel. It is not just that Beza knew of Coverdale's edition on this, Beza and Coverdale were personally associated together, as Coverdale also worked on the Geneva Bible. Beza clearly saw this reading here and most likely in Luther's translation, which in Exodus 3:14 the Luther Bible of 1545 in the Frühneuhochdeutsche:

> Ich werde sein, der **ich sein werde**.

Translated as:

> **I will be** who **I will be**.

The link between I AM and the "shalt be" reading can be clearly seen here.

3.15 1549 Ethipoic

The 1549 Ethiopic Bible

As pointed out by Hoskier in Concerning the Text of the Apokalypse[155], the Ethiopic bible reads "shalt be". This was first printed in Rome in 1549 and later in Walton's Polyglot of 1657. In the Nestle Aland Apparatus, it is known as the abbreviation "eth.ro" for Ethiopic/Rome.[156]

The below is from Walton's Ethiopic Bible, followed by a Latin interpretation of the Ethiopic.

Ethiopic 1549 in Walton's Polyglot

---

[155] https://archive.org/details/Hoskier-ConcerningTheTextOfTheApokalypse
[156] http://www.katapi.org.uk/UBSGrNT/Intro3.htm

in fontes aquarum: et facti sunt sanguis omnes fontes aquarum. Et dixit Ange- 5 lus fontium aquarum; Justus es Domine, et rectus, qui fuisti et eris, sic judica- sti eos: Quia effuderunt sanguinem Sanctorum tuorum et propherum...

Ethiopic 1549 translated into Latin in Walton's Polyglot

The date of the first version of ancient Ethiopic (Aethiopic, also known as Ge'ez and Amharic,) is not precisely known, but the fourth century is a common approximation. It has been judged that the first Ethiopic translation was made from the Greek language. In the picture below Herman Hoskier cites "and shalt be" in the Ethiopic Version with the following Latin translation:

...qui fuisti **et eris**

Which translates as:

....which has been and **shalt be**.

Justus es, Domine, et Rectus qui fuisti et eris *aeth.*

ὁ ων και ὁ ων (*pro* ο ων και ο ην) 32.   —και ο ην 167.   —και *ante* ὁ ην *sah.*

qui fuisti et futurus es *Beat.*   qui es et qui fuisti *Prim.*   [qui es et qui eras *h vg*].

Hoskier pointed out that the "aeth" Ethiopic, has "et futurus es" or "and shalt be".[157]

In the Preface to the King James Version in 1611, Miles Smith mentions how Chrysostom spoke concerning the Ethiopic:

So, S. Chrysostom that lived in S. Jerome's time, giveth evidence with him: "The doctrine of S. John [saith he] did not in such sort [as the Philosophers' did] vanish away: but the Syrians, Egyptians, Indians, Persians,

---

[157]   https://archive.org/stream/Hoskier-ConcerningTheTextOfTheApokalypse/Hoskier ApokalypseRevelation#page/n1233/mode/2up/search/eris

Ethiopians, and infinite other nations being barbarous people translated it into their [mother] tongue, and have learned to be [true] Philosophers,"

Smith later said:

So Postel affirmeth, that in his travel he saw the Gospels in the Ethiopian tongue; And Ambrose Thesius allegeth the Pslater of the Indians, which he testifieth to have been set forth by Potken in Syrian characters.

Many years before Christianity, Judaism was introduced to Ethiopia from the time of the visit of the Queen of Sheba to Solomon. Recent discoveries of manuscripts dating to the fourth to sixth centuries suggests the presence of Christianity before the fourth century, along with the possibility of Ge'ez translations. In the fourth century, Christianity had become the state religion, during the reign of King Ezana (first half of the fourth century), with St. Frumentius as bishop. Ge'ez itself changed, with the introduction of vowels and the reversal of the direction writing from right-to-left to left-to-right.

The Ethiopic version proves White wrong yet again. He claims no one knew of the reading, but this clearly shows that people did know it. It shows that 33 years before the word esomenos saw the ink of Beza it was sitting in Rome, in the Ethiopic bible at Revelation 16:5. But it seems that this information is not good enough for White who rashly claimed on his DL program that Beza didn't know of the reading. We shall examine this claim in the next chapter.

CHAPTER 4

Father, glorify thy name. Then came there a voice from heaven, saying, I have both glorified it, and will glorify it again. - John 12:28

James White said on his Dividing Line program concerning the 1549 Ethiopic bible with the reading of "shalt be":

> "...Couple of simple questions, did Beza have this information? Answer? No... So was Beza engaging in a conjectural Emendation? Yes..."[158]

4.1 Reformers: Tremellius, Junius, and Beza

White emphatically states that Beza didn't know of the Ethiopic reading. How he knows that, seeing he knows so little about any of the external or internal evidence for Revelation 16:5 reveals his presupposed anti TR/KJV position. He had his text, his tradition, and it seems no evidence will sway him from that.

---

[158] https://www.youtube.com/watch?v=Uqh4Jc2VkAM (from about the 25-minute mark)

In his translation process, Beza also made use of several ancient translations from editions prepared by Immanuel Tremellius who produced the Syriac and Franciscus Junius who produced the Arabic. Both of these scholars were experts in Hebrew, Aramaic, and its cognates of Syriac and Chaldee, as well as Arabic, Greek, and Latin. The first edition of the Tremellius/Junius Bible appeared in 1579 and after the death of Tremellius the version had several recensions by Junius. Three years after its publication, the Tremellius/Junius translation of the Old Testament was frequently paired as well with Theodore Beza's Latin translation of the New Testament which contained the eris/esomenos reading of Revelation 16:5. They considered Beza a world class expert on Greek and Latin, and utilized his version whenever they could. Junius was a significant Reformed Protestant voice who began to study under both Calvin and Beza from 1562. The Tremellius/Junius/Beza Bible shaped Protestant theology and dogmatics well into the late eighteenth century.

Theodore Beza (top), along with associates Junius (left) and Tremellius (right) who gave the reformation its best Latin Version

The Italian Jew John Immanuel Tremellius (1510–1580), converted to Catholicism in 1540 and then to Christianity the following year, during the period when he was a teacher of Hebrew at the monastic school at Lucca. Between 1530 and 1540. He had pursued classical studies at the University of Padua. Between 1549 and 1552 he was Professor of Hebrew at Cambridge University. He taught Hebrew in several locations in Europe during his lifetime. He was also the first person of that era to correctly distinguish between dialects of Aramaic, arguing that Syriac was not the dialect of Aramaic which was used by Jesus.

Catholics in Rome published the first edition of the Syriac New Testament in 1555. Before Tremellius, most scholars in Syriac were Roman Catholic. Tremellius would have watched closely and learned from them. The first Syriac bible should have been printed in Rome about 1548, but the scholars involved were busy on the Ethiopic bible of 1549. Tesso Zionis Malhesini (aka Peter Sionita) headed the Ethiopic project, and Marcello Cervini oversaw the project. Cervini was intimately involved in French politics as well as the Syriac bible. Cervini was later to become Pope, who reigned only twenty-two days, dying in 1555. Yet even during his short stint as Pope the Syriac bible was immediately commissioned to be printed, which under the previous Pope Julius III was forbidden to print. Moses of Mardin, who went on to print the Syrian bible, was associated with the two foremost Ethiopic scholars who worked on the Ethiopic New Testament, which was printed by the brothers Valerius Doricus and Ludovicus. Beza, like Cervini, was very entrenched in the local French politics of his day. I doubt Beza would not have known of the Ethiopic translation, as James White claims, seeing Marcello Cervini oversaw the project. I suppose White assumes that the only influences Beza must have had he would have written in his footnote, but Beza was very well connected with various translators, who knew of the Ethiopic. Beside the contemporaries of Beza's in Lausanne and Geneva, he had a large correspondence with many of the leading scholars of the time which aided his New Testament editions. For White to assert that Beza didn't know of the Ethiopic is pure speculation and is again another slanderous accusation he so quickly slanders Erasmus and the KJV translators with.

The great work of Tremellius was the translation of the Bible from Hebrew and Syriac into Latin, accomplished during his residence at Metz in about 1560. Tremellius' 1569 edition, using Hebrew script, appeared visually inferior than earlier Syriac editions, but sought to use historical linguistics to restore the phonetic vocalization of the Aramaic to its earliest form, a form considered closer to that of Jesus. Interestingly, Tremellius was good friends with Matthew Parker and Thomas Cranmer, and was godfather to Parker's son. Tremellius lived with Parker for nearly six months in 1565. Parker later became the principle translator of the Bishops bible in 1568. The Bishops Bible was the version the King James Translators were to base their work from 50 years later. Tremellius had written grammatical books that were published by Stephanus. He had a good relationship with Beza and Stephanus. In 1579, three years before Beza put esomenos into his Greek text, Tremellius published his text, and at Exodus 3:14 he has:

> id est **ero**, vel sum: futurum enimp pore ac presente usurpatur

which translates as:

> that is, **will be**, or I am: the future continuous time and the present used

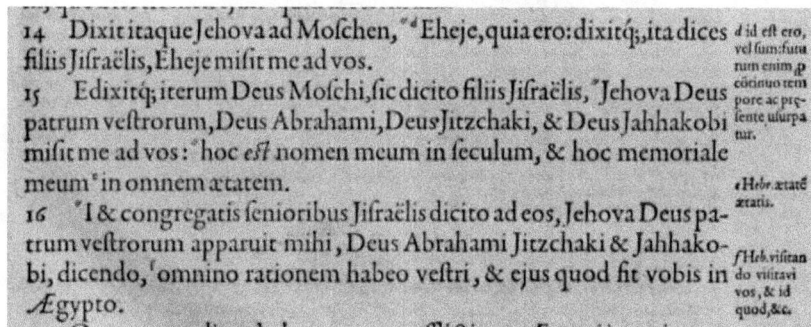

> 14 Dixit itaque Jehova ad Mofchen, "Eheje, quia ero: dixitq;, ita dices *d id eft ero,* filiis Jifraëlis, Eheje mifit me ad vos. *vel fum:futu rum enim,p*
>
> 15 Edixitq; iterum Deus Mofchi, fic dicito filiis Jifraëlis, "Jehova Deus *cōcinuo tem* patrum veftrorum, Deus Abrahami, Deus Jitzchaki, & Deus Jahhakobi *pore ac prç- fente ufurpa- tur.* mifit me ad vos: "hoc *eft* nomen meum in feculum, & hoc memoriale meum° in omnem ætatem. *e Hebr. ætatē ætatis.*
>
> 16 "I & congregatis fenioribus Jifraëlis dicito ad eos, Jehova Deus pa- trum veftrorum apparuit mihi, Deus Abrahami Jitzchaki & Jahhako- *f Heb. vifitan* bi, dicendo, °omnino rationem habeo veftri, & ejus quod fit vobis in *do viifitavi vos, & id* Ægypto. *quod, &c.*

Tremellius at Exodus 3:14 has "will be" in the footnote as Luther and Coverdale had.

In Beza's 1582 revision of the *Annotations*, his Latin and Greek translation was aided by Tremellius' edition. Many times in which textual variation is noted by Beza, the Syriac is mentioned. Beza stated that the Syriac was 'worthy of the highest authority'. Revelation was not included in Syriac in Tremellius' 1569 version so the Greek and Latin version of Beza was used there instead. Scholars of the time recognized the superior reading of *esomenos* over *osios* in that time period and the leading reformation period scholars such as Junius agreed with the reading.[159]

So why do I have this section about Juinus and Tremellius, their relationship to Beza, and their sphere of language knowledge? It is because James White has emphatically claimed that Beza didn't know of the Ethiopic reading at Revelation 16:5. Surprisingly the *Institut für neutestamentliche Textforschung* has recently made similar claims:

> There is some versional evidence (such as the Aethiopic), but Beza could not know about this.[160]

A latter edition of the Tremellius-Junius-Beza bible. Note the Tetragrammaton used twice on the page, which seems a rather fitting picture of the verse at hand. This later edition (post 1582) has eris, which is Latin for "shalt be" at Rev 16:5.

Well at least they now actually acknowledge the Ethiopic reading there and call it evidence, which is the exact opposite of White's response. I wonder if White

---

[159] http://www.juniusinstitute.org/about/junius/
[160] http://ntvmr.uni-muenster.de/nt-conjectures?conjID=cj10561

will now write a scathing report on the *Institut* for claiming this is actual evidence as I firstly did. Behold the double standards of White! Because the first Syriac bible should have been printed in Rome about 1548, but the scholars involved were busy on the Ethiopic bible of 1549, because Marcello Cervini oversaw the project, later to be the Pope (i.e. most powerful man in Europe at that time), who immediately commissioned the Syriac to be printed, and because Moses of Mardin who printed it, was associated with the two foremost Ethiopic scholars who worked on the Ethiopic, it seems like the "Beza didn't know of the Ethiopic" claim is false. In Syriac circles it would be almost impossible for these things to be unnoticed.

4.2 John Calvin

John Calvin, whom Theodore Beza succeeded in Geneva, usually used Jehovah in his Latin version that he prepared for his commentary on the Psalms of 1557. Pierre Robert Olivétan (1535) of Neuchâtel, who was also Calvin's cousin, while working on a French version used the expression *L'Éternel* which means "the Eternal One" to represent Jehovah in certain places. Eleven years later, the followers of Calvin in Geneva produced the French Geneva Bible of 1588 with similar readings. By translating Jehovah as *L'Éternel* it attempted to represent the Sacred Name according to the supposed meaning, "the One who exists eternally." We can see this concept in Calvin's quote concerning the I AM in Exodus 3:14 and 6:2:

> **I am who I am**. The verb in the Hebrew is in the future tense, "**I will be what I will be**;" but it is of the same force as the present, except that it designates the

perpetual duration of time. This is very plain, that God attributes to himself alone divine glory, because he is self-existent [sit a se ipso] and therefore **eternal**; and thus gives being [esse] and existence [subsistere] to every creature. Nor does he predicate of himself anything common, or shared by others; but he claims for himself eternity as peculiar to God alone, in order that he may be honored according to his dignity. Therefore, immediately afterwards, contrary to grammatical usage, he used the same verb in the first person as a substantive, annexing it to a verb in the third person; that our minds may be filled with admiration as often as his incomprehensible essence [essentiae] is mentioned. But although philosophers discourse in grand terms of this eternity, and Plato constantly affirms that God is peculiarly τὸ ὄν (the Being); yet they do not wisely and properly apply this title, viz., that this one and only Being of God absorbs all imaginable essences; and that, thence, at the same time, the chief power and government of all things belong to him. For from whence come the multitude of false gods, but from impiously tearing the divided Deity into pieces by foolish imaginations? Wherefore, in order rightly to apprehend the one God, we must first know, that all things in heaven and earth derive at His will their essence, or subsistence from One, who only truly is. From this Being all power is derived; because, if God sustains all things by his excellency, he governs them also at his will. ...

It would be tedious to recount the various opinions as to the name "**Jehovah**." It is certainly a foul superstition of the Jews that they dare not speak, or write it, but substitute the name "Adonai;" nor do I any more approve of their teaching, who say that it is ineffable, because it is not written according to grammatical rule. Without controversy, **it is derived from the word היה or הוה and therefore it is rightly said by learned commentators to be the essential name of God** [nomen essentiale Dei], whereas others are, as it were, epithets. Since, then, nothing is more peculiar to God than eternity, He is called Jehovah, because He has existence from Himself, and sustains all things by His secret inspiration. Nor do I agree with the grammarians, who will not have it pronounced, because its inflection is irregular; **because its etymology, of which all confess that God is the author, is more to me than an hundred rules.**[161]

Beza took the position in Geneva from Calvin when he died. He knew Calvin's work like no other. We can see from the above that Calvin would have had a massive influence on Revelation 16:5 in Beza's mind. "Will be" was the interpretation of Luther, Coverdale, and Calvin. Note also that Calvin linked Jehovah to *hava* and *hayah*, further disproving White's Twitter spray that this was not so.

This is also demonstrated in the 1560 Geneva Bible note at Exodus 3:14:

> The God which haue euer bene, am and **shalbe**: the God almightie, by whome all things haue their being, and the God of mercie mindeful of my promes, {Reuel 1:4}.

So we can see from the 1560 Geneva notes that **shalbe** was written. It also mentioned Revelation 1:4 which is the first of the Triadic Declarations. Théodore Beza himself, the most pre-eminent Greek and Hebrew scholar of his day, oversaw the work of the team, including Miles Coverdale and John Knox, that produced the Geneva Bible in 1557-60. Among the scholars who worked on the original Geneva bible was William Whittingham, who supervised the translation, in collaboration with Myles Coverdale, Christopher Goodman, Anthony Gilby, Thomas Sampson, and

---

[161]http://www.bible-researcher.com/tetragrammaton.html#note13

William Cole. Calvin, Knox, Beza, over 150 editions were issued; the last probably in 1644. In 1576 Tomson added L'Oiseleur's notes for the Epistles, which came from Beza's Greek and Latin edition of the Bible (1565 and later). Beginning in 1599 Franciscus Junius' notes on Revelation were added, replacing the original notes deriving from John Bale and Heinrich Bullinger.

4.3 Theodore Beza

The first trace of esomenos in Beza's readings is in Beza's own handwritten notes on his 1565 edition on page 647 in preparation for the third edition of 1582.[162]

ὁ ἐσόμενος was inserted into the main body of text in printed editions of the Textus Receptus by Theodore Beza in his 1582 edition.[163] One can see in Beza's hand copy that, ὁ ὅσιος and *Sanctus* are both underlined, and ὁ ἐσόμενος entered in the margin at that stage. There are about 200 Greek manuscripts in existence containing Revelation 16:5, but ὁ ἐσόμενος is lacking in all of them and the reading ὁ ὅσιος prevails. But as mentioned, only 4 Greek manuscripts of Revelation 16:5 exist from before the 10th century, and the 3 earliest witnesses of Revelation 16:5 do not even agree.

Beza saw this erroneous pattern below that disturbed the basic Triadic Declaration structure in his previous editions of the Greek New Testament:

---

[162] http://doc.rero.ch/record/18245?ln=fr
[163] http://ntvmr.uni-muenster.de/nt-conjectures?conjID=cj10561

ὁ	ὢν	καὶ	ὁ	ἦν	καὶ	ὁ	ἐρχόμενος	Rev 1:4
ὁ	ὢν	καὶ	ὁ	ἦν	καὶ	ὁ	ἐρχόμενος	Rev 1:8
ὁ	ἦν	καὶ	ὁ	ὢν	καὶ	ὁ	ἐρχόμενος	Rev 4:8
ὁ	ὢν	καὶ	ὁ	ἦν	καὶ	ὁ	ἐρχόμενος	Rev 11:17
ὁ	ὢν	καὶ	ὁ	ἦν	καὶ	ὁ	ὅσιος	Rev 16:5

And he replaced *ὅσιος* with *ἐσόμενος* in his 1582 edition:

ὁ	ὢν	καὶ	ὁ	ἦν	καὶ	ὁ	ἐρχόμενος	Rev 1:4
ὁ	ὢν	καὶ	ὁ	ἦν	καὶ	ὁ	ἐρχόμενος	Rev 1:8
ὁ	ἦν	καὶ	ὁ	ὢν	καὶ	ὁ	ἐρχόμενος	Rev 4:8
ὁ	ὢν	καὶ	ὁ	ἦν	καὶ	ὁ	ἐρχόμενος	Rev 11:17
ὁ	ὢν	καὶ	ὁ	ἦν	καὶ	ὁ	ἐσόμενος	Rev 16:5

Beza plainly saw that the Triadic Declaration is the Sacred Name of *Jehovah* in Revelation, not just as a phrase, but as a proper name, describing the eternality of the beginning, middle, and end of *Jehovah*; the past, present, and future, of the I AM, the "shalbe". The Revelation 16:5 footnote in Theodore Beza's 1588 says:

> "Et Qui eris, και ο εσομενος": The usual publication is "και ο οσιος," which shows a division, contrary to the whole phrase which is foolish, distorting what is put forth in scripture. The Vulgate, however, whether it is articulately correct or not, is not proper in making the change to "οσιος, Sanctus," since a section (of the text) has worn away the part after "και," which would be absolutely necessary in connecting "δικαιος" and "οσιος." But with John there remains a completeness where the name of Jehovah (the Lord) is used, just as we have said before, 1:4; he always uses the three closely together, therefore it is certainly "και ο εσομενος," for why would he pass over it in this place? And so without doubting the genuine writing in this ancient manuscript, I faithfully

restored in the good book what was certainly there, "o εσομενος." So why not truthfully, with good reason, write "ο ερχομενος" as before in four other places, namely 1:4 and 8; likewise in 4:8 and 11:17, because the point is the just Christ shall come away from there and bring them into being: in this way he will in fact appear sitting in judgment and exercising his just and eternal decrees.[164]

Beza claims that the reading of "and holy" caused a division between the words and that it made the reading "foolish, distorting what is put forth in scripture." Beza was not alone, Valla and Erasmus both questioned the verse and offered alternative readings in their annotations. The *foolish and divisional* reading is demonstrated in English versions:

1395 [And the thridde aungel... seide,] Just art thou, Lord, that art, **and that were hooli**, that demest these thingis; (Wycliffe)

1526 And I herde an angell saye: lorde which arte and **wast thou arte ryghteous and holy** because thou hast geve soche iudgmentes (Tyndale)

1535 And I herde an angel saye: LORDE which art and wast, **thou art righteous and holy**, because thou hast geue soche iudgmentes, (Coverdale)

1557 And I heard the Angel of the waters say, Lord, thou art iust, Which art, and **Which wast: and Holy**, because thou hast iudged these things. (Geneva)

1568 And I hearde the angell of the waters say: Lorde, which art, and wast, **thou art ryghteous & holy**, because thou hast geuen such iudgementes: (Bishop's)

So as we can see, early English translators were very perplexed as to how to fit καὶ ὁ ὅσιος into their versions. Beza replaced the illogical language found in earlier

---

[164] (Theodore Beza, Nouum Sive Nouum Foedus Iesu Christi, 1588. Translated into English from the Latin footnote.)

Greek texts/manuscripts and knew that "and holy" or "the holy one" interrupts the continuity of reference to God's eternal name of Jehovah/I AM, and omits a predictable logical third verb of "shalt be". Beza's rendering speaks of the eternal God of the past, present & future, as expected of a true reading, and in accord with Revelation 1:4, 8; 4:8; & 11:17. All five of the Revelation verses present the obvious expected future aspect of God's eternality. The "I AM" is the "shalbe". Beza claimed that the reading of "holy" was *distorting what is put forth in scripture*. Beza was well aware of the manuscript evidence and said:

> The Vulgate, however, whether it is articulately correct or not, is not proper in making the change to "οσιος, Sanctus," since a section (of the text) has worn away the part after "και," which would be absolutely necessary in connecting "δικαιος" and "οσιος.".

Beza knew that Latin manuscripts and versions had attempted to harmonize the nomina sacra reading of "holy" into the text, and had failed in doing so. The Vulgate connected *Righteous* with *Holy*, but Beza knew that the necessary reading after και (and) needed to be there. The Vulgate was much like P47 which included the AND before "holy". And although White claims it was firstly seen in the 1598, the first time Beza placed εσομενος *and eris* into print was in 1582. Beza well knew that the *usual publication is "και ὁ ὅσιος,"* and that both the Greek and Latin manuscripts had *ὅσιος and sanctus*. Beza clearly notes he used ἐσόμενος because of the connection to the reading of Jehovah:

> But with John there remains a completeness where the name of Jehovah (the Lord) is used, just as we have said before, 1:4; he always uses the three closely together, therefore it is certainly "και ο εσομενος," for why would he pass over it in this place?

Beza knowing the style of John, with his propensity to reveal "I AM" in the gospels and Jehovah to the Triadic Declaration in Revelation, expressly said that where Jehovah is used in context, the Triadic Declaration follows, and that readers should look at what Beza had formerly said in Revelation 1:4. So at Revelation 16:5 in Beza's footnotes in his 1582, 1588, & 1598 Greek and Latin New Testament, and also 1594 Annotations, all clearly point to a preceding footnote in Revelation 1:4. I doubt James White has even bothered to read the rest of the footnote in Revelation 16:5 beyond his sound bite *"ex vetusto bonae fidei manuscripto codice restitui"*, *"I faithfully restored in the good book what was certainly there"*, and thus didn't follow Beza's recommendation to go the Revelation 1:4 where he had the information about the Triadic Declaration and the link to the sacred names Jehovah and I AM. Nor do I think White knew or understood the concepts Beza was saying here in the slightest. As mentioned earlier, although Daniel Wallace is flawed on many levels concerning his understanding of textual criticism, he provides this excellent example that fits here:

> "Imagine we came across an early manuscript copy of the Constitution of the United States, and the preamble said, "We the people of the United States, in order to form a more perfect onion ..." If we were to see that line, we would know that "union" was the original word, not "onion"."[165]

After Beza had spoken about his certainty of the connection between Jehovah, and the Triadic

---

[165] *Is the Original New Testament Lost? Ehrman vs Wallace (Debate Transcript)* http://www.credocourses.com/blog/2016/original-new-testament-lost-ehrman-vs-wallace-debate-transcript/

Declaration, and how the abrupt reading of "holy" fails in both Greek and Latin, and the precedent of John's four earlier examples, he then states:

> And so without doubting the genuine writing in this ancient manuscript, I faithfully restored in the good book what was certainly there, "ο εσομενος."

He then speaks concerning the five editions of Erasmus in his *Annotations*, which said "who is, who was, who is to come", ὁ ὤν, ὁ ἦν ὁ ἐρχόμενος:

> So why not truthfully, with good reason, write "ο ερχομενος" as before in four other places, namely 1:4 and 8; likewise in 4:8 and 11:17, because the point is the just Christ shall come away from there and bring them into being: in this way he will in fact appear sitting in judgment and exercising his just and eternal decrees.

Beza, with the precedence of 5th century Jerome reading of "and shalt be", the 8th century Beatus reading of "and will be", the 9th century Haimo reading of "shalt be", the 1549 Ethiopic translation reading of "shalt be", the καὶ ὁ ἐσόμενος reading of Clement in the 3rd Century relating to Jehovah, the Tremellius, Junius, and Calvin, definition of I AM and Jehovah being "shalt be", as also Luther and Coverdale, who at Exodus 3:14 read "will be", he also looked to the context of the verse, that the second coming was the very next thing, and chose ὁ ἐσόμενος over Erasmus' ὁ ἐρχόμενος. Although he did admit, that Erasmus had good reason to choose ὁ ἐρχόμενος, Beza having mused upon these concepts for many years, using Erasmus' ceiling as his platform, elected "shalt be", and for good reason!

Beza was also saying he faithfully restored the kai, but rejected the osios.

"Et Qui eris, και ο εσομενος": The usual publication is "και ο οσιος,"

White claims that Beza rejected the reading of ο οσιος, but that is wrong, it was clearly **και** ο οσιος. White would do well to examine the reformation scholars who agreed with Beza and promoted the model such as Johannes Piscator in 1613, and Sebastian Benefield in 1629, and Erasmus Schmidius in 1658, who are but a few examples.

Concerning Beza's conclusion of ἐσόμενος vs ἐρχόμενος Spiros Zodhiates in his *The Complete Word Study Dictionary New Testament* has in his lengthy explanation of the Triadic Declaration at number 3801 which mentions:

> "...The events described under the figure of bowls in Rev. 16 occur at the end of the Great Tribulation and take a very short time, maybe only a few days. Therefore the Lord Jesus is no more described as ho *erchómenos* (the coming One) as before, but as the One about to be here..."[166]

5 And I heard the Angell of the waters say, Lord, thou artiust, Which art, and Which waſt, and Which ſhalt be; becauſe thou haſt iudged theſe things.

Revelation 16:5 in the 1594 English translation of Junius Franciscus.
After 1582, the reading was in all of Junius' editions as the 1611 KJV has it.

It is of interest that in Revelation 16:5 in the latter

[166] Spiros Zodhiates in his The Complete Word Study Dictionary New Testament Page 1086. 1993 Revised edition by AMG International, Inc.

Arabic bible in Walton's Polyglot of 1657, it is translated as "Aeterne" in Latin, which is the eternal One of eternity past, present, and future, or I AM.

الاَبْنَاءُ كُلُّهَا دَمًا *فَسَمِعْتُ مَلاَكَ المِيَاهِ يَقُولُ عَدْلٌ هُوَ أَنْتَ الأَزَلِيُّ الصَّفِيُّ اَوِ حَكَمْتَ هَكَذَا فِي ٥
هَؤُلاَءِ * الَّذِينَ أَهْرَقُوا دَمَ القِدِّيسِينَ وَالأَنْبِيَاءِ وَجَعَلْتَهُمْ يَشْرَبُونَ الدَّمَ كَمَا هُوَ اسْتِحْقَاقُهُمْ ٦

Walton's Arabic

sæque sunt aquæ omnes in sanguinem. Et 5
audivi Angelum aquarum dicentem,
Justus es tu Æterne, Electissime, quod
hæc judicaveris in eos. Qui effude- 6

Walton's Latin translation of the Arabic

4.4 King James Version Translators

5 And J heard the Angel of the waters say, Thou art righteous, O Lord, which art, and was, and shalt be, because thou hast iudged thus:

Lets look at the people that White suspects of making the erroneous decision to follow the reading of Beza by introducing "shalt be" into the KJV. The legendary scholarship of the 1611 translators includes the Second Oxford Company, who translated the Book of Revelation, the Gospels, and Acts. The linguistic, scholarly, and church experience of the members of his company was unequaled which included Thomas Ravis, George Abbot, Richard Eedes, Giles Tomson, Sir Henry Savile, John Peryn, Ralph Ravens, John Harmar, John Aglionby, and Leonard Hutten. Their translation was reviewed by the members of each of the other five companies. Thus it can be said that the final product in Revelation 16:5, was collectively agreed upon.

People such as John Bois, Lancelot Andrewes, George Abbot (who also replaced Bancroft after his death) are rather well known today as the leading scholars of that period. In my article *Why we should not Passover Easter Part 1*, I wrote about the scholarship of Henry Saville:

> Henry Saville was famous for his Greek and mathematical learning at a young age. He was Queen Elizabeth's tutor in Greek and Mathematics. He translated countless ancient works from Latin and Greek his chief work being the first to edit the complete work of Chrysostom, the most famous of the Greek church fathers, in eight large folios. A folio was the size of a large dictionary or encyclopaedia.

In my second article *Why we should not Passover Easter Part 2*, I wrote concerning Saville:

> He was an expert on the Greek language, mathematics, and church history and had been the personal tutor in Greek and mathematics to Queen Elizabeth. He also founded the first chairs of Geometry and Astronomy in Oxford. His greatest work, besides his work on the King James Bible, was translating the complete works of the most famous Greek Church father John Chrysostom from Greek into English. During his compilation of 15,800 manuscript sheets, he scoured all the great Libraries of Europe, buying the oldest and purest of the Chrysostom manuscripts. Savile's edition of Chrysostom has been called "the one great work of

162

Renaissance scholarship carried out in England", and was the most considerable work of pure learning undertaken in England at that time.

Saville would stand alone as an expert on this issue, but some others in the company were:

John Harmar obtained the regius professorship of Greek at Oxford. He held this position for five years. In Geneva, he attended lectures of Beza. He published an English translation of Beza's sermons, he debated with Catholic theologians in Paris. He was responsible for the first Greek book printed at Oxford, consisting of several sermons of Church Father John Chrysostom. He has been called a "most noble Latinist and Grecian". He was one of three known men who were asked to serve on the committee of reviewers and revisers of the entire bible with John Bois and Andrew Downes. These men went through the entire Bible, checking the translation, resolving issues raised by the companies, and spotting concerns arising for the first time and dealing with them. This review took nine months to complete according to John Bois.

John Aglionby was described as "a person well accomplished in all kinds of learning, profoundly read in the Fathers, and in school divinity, and exact linguist." According a biographer "He was esteemed one of the greatest students of the Greek language of any that lived in that age, and kept correspondence with learned men in every part of the Christian world."

John Perin as a veteran Greek reader and regius professor of Greek was one of the most experienced and esteemed Greek scholars in England if not in all Europe. He resigned his college readership in order to devote time to the AV translation, demonstrating his commitment to the translation project.

Robert Fludd, who became a prominent physician, mathematician, cosmologist and astrologer, was tutored by John Perin while a student at St. John's College, Oxford. Leonard Hutten, described as "an excellent Grecian". In 1602 he was called upon to officiate at the opening of the Bodleian Library. A year later, Leonard Hutten was named pro-vice-chancellor of the university. He wrote historical accounts of both his college and of Oxford. Even KJV translator Richard Brett was eminent as a linguist in Latin, Greek, Hebrew, Chaldee, Arabic, and ***Ethiopic***.[167]

The above men, and many others, are slandered by White as buffoons who slipped on a banana peel and goofed up. He keeps claiming that these deceptive dummies just followed a conjecture. But his slander does not end there. He also slanders the Dutch bible translators and Elzevir.

4.5 Dutch Statenvertaling

Most reformers were Jehovist and knew the importance and significance of the Sacred Name of God. This is the 1637 Dutch Statenvertaling which has the same reading as Beza and the Authorized Version:

> En ik hoorde den engel der wateren zeggen: Gij zijt rechtvaardig, Heere! Die is, en Die was, **en Die zijn zal**, dat Gij dit geoordeeld hebt;

Translated to read:

> And I heard the angel of the waters say, Thou art righteous, O Lord! Who is and who was **and who will be**, because thou hast judged;

---

[167] http://kingjamesbibletranslators.org/bios/Richard_Brett/

Cude ich hoozde den Engel des watcren feggen/
Bhn zijt rechtveerdigh/ Heere/ Die is/ ende Die was/
ende Die zijn fal/ dat ghp dit geoordeelt hebt :

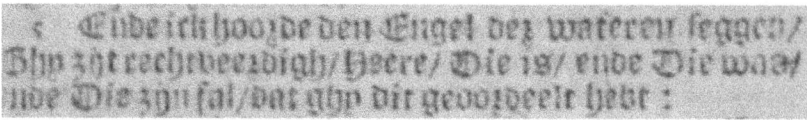

The Original spelling of the 1637

The 1637 Dutch Statenvertaling which is renowned to be an equivalent of the King James Version in the Dutch language, has the same reading of Beza and the KJV in Revelation 16:5.

The Statenvertaling (States-General) Bible stems from the Synod of Dort, 1618-19 which was a meeting where many representatives attended who had links to Beza and also the KJV translation, such as Authorized Version translators Lancelot Andrewes, Samuel Ward, and Giovanni Diodati who succeeded Beza from Geneva the Chair of theology at the Genevan Academy, and many other international scholars. From 19–27 November 1618, seven sessions were devoted to Bible translation questions. It was unanimously decided that there was need for a new Bible translation into Dutch. The Statenvertaling Six translators were appointed to the work, three for the Old Testament and three for the New Testament and Apocrypha. There were two Frieslanders, two East Flemings, one Zeelander and one Hollander (the province, not the nation). They had also been provided with access to the necessary scholarly help and a good library. The example of the recent English Authorized Version of 1611 was to be followed for preciseness and accuracy. In Revelation 16:5, they followed the 1633 Greek reading of Elzevir which is the same reading as Beza's 1582. The translators stated that the meaning of Jehovah was "the independent/ self being/ being the same from eternity to eternity/ and the origin or cause of existence of all things":

> Na de voleyndinge van het werck der scheppinge/ wort hier aldereerst Gode de naem van IEHOVAH gegeven/ beteeckenende de selfstandigen/ selfwesenden/ van hem selven zijnde van eeuwicheyt tot eeuwicheyt/ ende den oorspronck ofte oorsake van het wesen aller dinge; daerom oock dese naem de ware Godt alleen toecomt. Onthoudt dit eens voor al; waer ghy voortae het woort HEERE met groote letteren geschreven vindt/ dat aldaer in 't Hebr. het woort IEHOVAH, oft korter/ IAH state.

Translated as:

> After the completion of the works of creation/ here for the first time God is given the name IEHOVAH/ meaning the independent/ self being/ being the same from eternity to eternity/ and the origin or cause of existence of all things; that is why this name only belongs to God. Remember for all time; wherever you from now on see the word LORD written in capital letters/ that there in Hebr. the word IEHOVAH, or shorter/ IAH is stated.

Translators were Johannes Bogerman, Willem Baudartius, and Gerson Bucerus for the Old Testament, and Jakobus Rolandus, Herman Faukelius, and Petrus Cornelisz for the New Testament and apocrypha. Herman Faukelius and Petrus Cornelisz died before they could start on the translation and were therefore replaced by Festus Hommius and Antonius Walaeus. Walaeus had studied under Franciscus Junius and spent much time in Geneva. Bogerman had personally met with Beza in 1598.

The Statenvertaling Bible Like many bibles of the era, the name Jehovah is at the top of the title page.

The Statenvertaling was written with specific guidelines for translation established by the Synod during its 8th session on November 20, 1618. The four main instructions to the translators were:

> That they always carefully adhere to the original text, and that the manner of writing of the original languages be preserved, as much as the clarity and properties of Dutch speech permit. But in case where the Hebrew or Greek manner of speech was harder than could remain in the text, that they note this in the margin.

> That they add as few words as possible to complete the meaning of a sentence if it is not expressed fully, and that these words be distinguished from the text with a different font and placed between brackets.

> That they formulate a short and clear summary for each book and chapter and write this in the margin at the respective locations in the Holy Scriptures.

> That they add a brief explanation providing insight to the translation of unclear passages; but the addition of lessons learnt is neither necessary nor advisable.

Notice the Dutch bible offered no explanation in a footnote for Revelation 16:5, just as the KJV translators did not, revealing their confidence in the reading of esomenos in the Elzevirs 1633 text, reflecting Beza's earlier reading of 1582. White seems to feel that the crowning Bible version of the Dutch and English language somehow slipped on a banana peel and goofed on this issue. The pinnacle of learning, the cream of the crop of the reformation along with all the 1611 translators, was again, a blunder, and a total goof up.

4.6 Elzevir's Editions

The 1624 edition of the Elzevirs' Greek text has "ὅσιος" but after much scholarly consideration the latter 1633 Elzevir text changed to the Beza reading of "ἐσόμενος", "shalt be"!

αἷμα. Καὶ ἤκυσα τῷ ἀγγέλυ τῶν ὑδά- 5 των λέγοντ@· Δίκαι@, Κύριε, εἶ, ὁ ὢν, &
ὁ ἦν, & ὁ ὅσιος, ὅτι ταῦτα ἔκρινας· Ὅτι αἷ- 6

The 1624 Greek edition of the Elzevir's has ho osios. Following Stephanus.

5 Καὶ ἤκυσα ᾗ ἀγγέλυ τ ὑδάτων λέγοντ@· Δίκαι@, Κύριε, εἶ, ὁ ὢν, κỳ ὁ ἦν, καὶ ὁ ἐσόμ@, ὅτι ταῦτα ἔκρινας·

The 1633 Greek edition of Elzevir's has ho esomenos exactly as Beza has it. Thus coming to terms with Beza's reasoning and evidence.

Gill's Exposition in Psalm 83:18 says:

> *That men may know that thou, whose name alone is JEHOVAH, art the most high over all the earth.*

Or, "that thou, thy name alone is **Jehovah**" (p), a self-existent Being, the Being of beings, **the everlasting I AM**, the immutable God; for this name is expressive of the being, eternity, and unchangeableness of God, **who**

is, and was, and is to come, invariably the same, **Revelation 1:4** which is to be understood not to the exclusion of the Son or Spirit, who are with the Father **the one Jehovah**, Deuteronomy 6:4, and to whom this name is given; see Exodus 17:6, compared with 1 Corinthians 10:9, Isaiah 6:8 compared with Acts 28:25, but to the exclusion of all nominal and fictitious deities, the gods of the Heathens; and the being and perfections of God are known by the judgments he executes, Psalm 9:16...

CONCLUSION

Heaven and earth shall pass away: but my words
shall not pass away -Mark 13:31

Let's finish with a quote from White in the *King James
Only Controversy*:

> Thankfully, there isn't the slightest doubt as to what
> John wrote here, and only misguided dedication to a
> human tradition would cause anyone to believe
> otherwise. Christians are people of truth, and I truly
> exhort any KJV Only advocate to seriously consider this
> text, to examine the documentation provided, and to
> recognize King James Onlyism for what it is: and
> unfounded tradition that flies in the face of the truth. [168]

Do you think there is not the "slightest doubt"
concerning Revelation 16:5 after reading this book? Do
you think the conclusions of this book are misguided,
just mere human tradition, or deceptive? Let's evaluate
the main points:

• Jehovah comes from "to be" and is related to the
Triadic Declaration (White denied this on Twitter)
• Jesus, who "is to come/shalt be" is Jehovah
• I AM also means "who is, and was, and shalt be"
• I AM in English bible versions shows "shalt be" is a
reasonable reading
• Hutter has "shalt be" in his Hebrew edition with "is to
come" in his Greek
• The NT Hebrew of Hutter at Revelation 16:5 is akin to
hava "to be"

---

[168] White, James. The King James Only Controversy: Can You Trust the Modern
Translations? (Updated June 1, 2009 Expanded edition), Minneapolis: Bethany House
Publishers; Updated, Paperback: 368 pages, p. 241, ISBN-13: 978-0764206054

• Most commentaries concerning the Triadic Declaration relate it to Jehovah and I AM
• The Triadic Declaration is a complete name with it's own Strong's number
• The "holy" in the manuscripts is a form of nomina sacra
• The Triadic Declaration is the *original* sacred name
• P47 has the "and" that Beza pointed to, which was going on to fulfill the triad
• Jerome has "shalt be" in the Triadic Declaration
• Clement of Alexandria speaking of Jehovah used "esomenos" knowing the correct NT reading of Revelation 16:5
• Gregory of Nyssa calls Christ the "esomenos"
• Beatus of Liébana has "shalt be" in both his Vulgate text *and also* in his commentary
• Haimo Halberstadensis has "shalt be" in his commentary
• Desiderius Erasmus has the Triadic Declaration as "is to come" in his Annotations in all five editions
• Luther, Coverdale, and Calvin had "will be" for "I AM" in Exodus 3:14
• The Ethiopic of 1549 has "shalt be" at Revelation 16:5
• Tremellius and Junius shared editions with Beza, and their edition adopted Beza's "shalt be" reading as soon as it came out in 1582
• John Calvin defined Jehovah and I AM as the Triadic Declaration
• Theodore Beza explained in his 1582 footnote that the Triadic Declaration appears when Jehovah appears
• The KJV translators did not slavishly follow Beza (see John 8:6; Acts 16:7) but chose to adopt "shalt be" knowing that Beza was correct
• The KJV translators left no note or italic (in John 2:23 they placed the reading in italics to show minority reading) showing they did not consider it a minority reading

• The Dutch Statenvertaling also independently chose the reading and left no italic or footnote
• James White says the pronunciation of Jehovah is false and Yahweh is true, against the basic facts
• James White in the Jack Moormon debate claimed that nomina sacra was originally designed to *save space* in manuscripts
• James White claimed Beza changed the reading "to make it nice and poetic and rhythmic" but failed to reveal the link to Jehovah, I AM, and how it is a complete formula of the most holy name of God[169]

• James White claimed "there's not a question about it on anyone's part as to what that passage actually reads", but many questioned it, from Erasmus (even Lorenzo Valla thought it was part of a Trinitarian Formula) through to the KJV translators' Elzevir's etc
• James White said Beza simply made the reading up - "why should I take Theodore Beza's conjectural emendation where he decides a reading on the basis of what he likes" and "the King James Version contains a reading created out of the mind of Theodore Beza"
• James White said "nobody before Theodore Beza ever had the idea that Revelation 16:5 read that way", and "was unknown to the ancient church, unknown to *all* Christians until the end of the sixteenth century", but many people thought it read that way
• James White claimed "Every Greek text – not just Alexandrian texts, but all Greek texts, Majority Text, the Byzantine text, every manuscript, the entire manuscript tradition – reads O Holy One," but as we have seen, the "Kai" is totally neglected and the manuscripts are not in agreement. White should have had "holy" or "and holy", not just "O Holy One"

---

[169] The King James Controversy Revisited - 2002, on the Ankerberg show, with Dr. Kenneth Barker, Dr. Don Wilkins, Dr. Daniel B. Wallace, Dr. James White, Dr. Samuel Gipp, Dr. Thomas Strouse, Dr. Joseph Chambers.

• James White said "Beza believed there was sufficient similarity between the Greek terms ὅσιος and ἐσόμενος (the future form, "shall be") to allow him to make the change to harmonize the text with other such language in Revelation." But it is very clear that Beza changed the text due to several *other* reasons, not because "osios" and "esomenos" had similar Greek lettering, revealing his ignorance of Beza's *Annotations*

• James White said "the King James Version reading at Revelation 16:5 arose from Theodore Beza's conjectural emendation *and was unknown to history prior to that time"* revealing White is totally ignorant of the evidence

• James White said "Tischendorf's notes on the term only confirm my assertion. He notes that "cop aeth" omit ὁ ὅσιος, but the KJV reading is not to be found even here, as ἐσόμενος is not put in its place." But when he rebuked me on his Dividing Line program in 2016, he specifically said that he was talking about the *Greek* here. So was White looking for the *Greek* word ἐσόμενος in the Coptic Ethiopic ("cop aeth") he mentions here? Is he claiming that the Ethiopic needed Greek lettering here? Clearly the Ethiopic in fact *does* indeed have the reading of "shalt be". He is either not understanding what "cop aeth" actually means, or was ignorant of the reading in the Ethiopic and being exposed that the Ethiopic does have it, he is now trying to claim the footnote is speaking of the Greek only, instead of saying he made a mistake

• James White said "Likewise, Hoskier's massive work on the text of the Apocalypse nowhere indicates the appearance of Beza's conjecture." But Hoskier clearly has "shalt be", but not in Greek. White has claimed many times that there is *no evidence at all.* Why didn't he mention the other evidence for the reading? Why not say there is no exact Greek reading, but it is in church commentaries, Ethiopic et al?

• James White said, "Quite simply, before Beza, no Christian had ever read the text the way the KJV has it today." So White is either saying Jerome, Beatus, and many others are not Christians or else he is totally *ignorant* about the evidence for this reading

So as we can see from the above points, White is completely wrong. His research is flawed and has caused massive confusion concerning this verse. The mountain of evidence shows *all* readings, including those reading "holy" point to the KJV reading. The nomina sacra point to Jehovah/I AM. Even if Beza's reasoning is rejected *against* the massive amount of evidence provided, "shalt be" is most certainly the second most attested reading from the external evidence shown. Because White has slandered those who rationally believe that world class experts actually knew what they were doing in the process of translating the best bible translation ever, I think he should officially apologize to the church for his ignorance and misinformation. Look at the slanderous accusations he makes:

> Thankfully, there isn't the slightest doubt as to what John wrote here, and only **misguided dedication to a human tradition would cause anyone to believe otherwise**. Christians are people of truth, and I truly exhort any KJV Only advocate to seriously consider this text, to examine the documentation provided, and to recognize King James Onlyism for what it is: **an unfounded tradition that flies in the face of the truth**.

Also:

> John **did not** write "and shalt be." He wrote "O Holy One." This is **the united testimony of all relevant historical information. To deny this is to engage in the most**

egregious form of irrational thought. It is not faith to deny reality, it is deception.

Mr White, you are totally out of line, unprofessional, unscholarly, ignorant, and a blight to the church. I will gladly debate you on this issue.

APPENDIX 1

Here is a transcript of what White said on the Dividing Line on September 1st 2016 upon finding my article (which can be also watched on youtube[170]). While many may find this a storm in a teacup, it brings into context the entire reason for this book and you will then understand why certain evidences are shown, to answer White's claims below:

> "Just today, an article was posted at textusreceptusbibles@blogspot.com... this is an awesome teaching opportunity. Some of the best teaching opportunities I have ever seen have come when someone thought they were refuting me. And when I get an opportunity to go "well, this is why you didn't refute me", it can sometimes give the greatest light. An article was posted called *Beza Vindicated*, I think this is an Australian writer by the name of Nick Sayers, I'm assuming this anyways, Nick Sayers, director of Textus Receptus... "I am currently living in Pakistan working on an Urdu Bible translation from the Textus Receptus" - that's just what they need, is an Urdu bible based upon a text that contains *errors* in it, that's just exactly what they needed. So that's great. And this article is Beza Vindicated quotes me concerning Revelation 16:5. Now, I did, in the current edition in the King James Only Controversy, I spent quite some time on Revelation 16:5, and I did so because I needed to introduce folks to the concept of conjectural emendation, and the fact that *by Theodore Beza's own confession*, he introduced a textual conjecture in Revelation 16:5. He did not have access to any Greek manuscript that read the way that he ended up putting his text in the printed edition of his text, in his 1598 text. And I provided pictures, most of the pictures appear here. and I even knew that there were going to be people who try to get around this, even when

---

[170] http://www.aomin.org/aoblog/2016/09/page/3/ From about the 25 minute mark.

I did this, because I said on page 240, as one can see the King James Version reading of revelation 16:5 arose from Theodore Beza's conjectural emendation and was unknown to history prior to that time. And I give a footnote: Lest in desperation a King James only advocate make the attempt, Tischendorf 's notes on the term only confirm my assertion. He notes that: C-o-p a-e-t-h* two different phrases, omit *ho hosios*, but the KJV reading is not to be found even here, as *esomenos*, (and this *ho hosios* is the holy one, and *esomenos* is the future form of the particle of the verb of being so, will be) is not put in it's place, instead Tischendorf's notes indicate Beza as the reading source.

Further, Tregelles' text indicate some translations omit *ho hosios* again indicates the KJV reading is nowhere in the *Greek* manuscript tradition. Likewise, Hoskier's massive work on the text the Apocalypse nowhere indicates the appearance of Beza's conjecture, quite simply, before Beza, no Christian had ever read the reading the way the KJV has it today. And I was obviously, in light of the pictures, and what I was talking about the Greek text, not English translations or things like that, the Greek text.

Well, various folks since then have done their best to try to come up with some way around this reality, and I remember someone saying, "well you know, there could have been manuscripts that we don't have anymore", and someone said "well you know, there's a commentary that mentions a Latin manuscript that has passed away" and so on and so forth... And I try to point out to these folks, don't you realize you are proving my point for me? On the one hand you will use Byzantine priority argumentation, or you'll use majority text argumentation, and yet, then you'll turn around, and to substantiate any place where the TR departs from either the Byzantine text or what would be called the Majority Text depending on which text we're talking about, whether you are talking about Robinson-Pierpont, Hodges Farstad, etc, etc. Then all of a sudden, all those arguments go out the window, and for this one verse, all of a sudden, a vague reference to a Latin manuscript someplace is enough to be the one place where the original was maintained. I have more respect for people who say "you know what, God re-inspired the Greek, He took over Erasmus, well actually in this case he took over Beza, He took over Erasmus and did a little bit, and took over Stephanus and did a little bit, then finally He takes over for Beza, and then basically, providentially guides supernaturally the selections of readings by the King James Translators between 1604 and 1611". At least those folks are consistent. Because they're not trying to pretend that there's actually a textual basis for this argumentation. They are saying "you know what, this is my text, God said it, God did it, I'm not going to bother with the manuscripts and all the rest of that stuff, it's all supernatural and yes, I know that put's me on the same level as Joseph Smith's inspired translation or other things like that, but that's what I am gonna say. At least I can go, there you go. I appreciate that you're not pretending to do something that you're not doing. The problem is now there is even a bunch of Calvinists, and you know who you are, who want to pretend that they are being confessional, in defending every reading of the Textus Receptus, including Beza's conjectural emendation. That this is what it means to be confessional you see.

Well, by the way I would like to invite you guys, especially to read a little book here by Jan Krans, Beyond What is Written - Erasmus and Beza as conjectural Critics of the New Testament. Very interesting to look at how many places Erasmus, and Beza, together, engaged in textual emendation in the production of the text that ended up producing the Textus Receptus. Interesting stuff there, lots of interesting material there.

Well, what do we have in this new article that just came out today...

"Well Mr James White, it looks like Theodore Beza wasn't the first to have "and shalt be" (ἐσόμενος) at Revelation 16:5." And then there's a graphic: "Revelation 16:5 in the 1549 Ethiopic Geez bible." Now remember I was talking about the Greek. So we have an Ethiopic bible, and then you have Brian Walton, a English priest, divine and scholar, with a polyglot in Revelation 16:5 his 1549 Ethiopian, known today as Amharic and formerly as Ge'ez version has a Latin translation with the words "et eris" you will be. So basically what is being said is, here's the specifics, the Ethiopic version as cited by Hermon Hoiskier in Latin, so the Ethiopic version, one, Ethiopic version, as cited in Latin.

Couple of simple questions, did Beza have this information? Answer? No... So was Beza engaging in a conjectural Emendation? Yes... Are you actually arguing for the supremacy of the Ethiopic over the Greek of the New Testament? Do you realize what this would mean to the rest of the New Testament? If you were to make the Ethiopic... are you actually arguing that the original was lost but only maintained in the Ethiopic?

See I've mentioned a number of times in dealing with Roman Catholic apologists on the subject of Sola Scriptura vs Sola Ecclesia, that the more the Roman Catholic struggles to get away from the reality of Sola Ecclesia the more they are entrapped within it. The more desperate they become. Well in this situation, those who attempt to defend the Textus Receptus, while pretending that they're doing textual criticism, end up demonstrating their own unbelievable desperation. Abject desperation. And here is a great example of it. Think about the argumentation that the TR folks use for Revelation 16:5, and then the Comma Johanneum, and then the Pericope Adulterae. So in other words, Revelation 16:5, what we are looking at right now, whether it's "the Holy One" or "and shall be", the first John 5:7, the Comma Johanneum, and then the Pericope Adulterae, the woman taken in Adultery, think about the form of argumentation that is presented on each one of these texts to defend them. And what you will recognize, what you are forced to recognize is that they are abjectly contradictory to one another, that they are ad hoc, there is no consistency, you could never have created a textual critical methodology that, then applied to the manuscripts, would come up with the Textus Receptus, you couldn't do it. The TR developed over time, it was an accident of history. You have to look at what Erasmus had available to him, what Stephanus had available to him, what Beza had available to them, the differences in understanding of textual criticism, the rise of Islam, the fall of Constantinople, there's just all sorts of things that just led into the creation of the Textus Receptus. The point is, there is no consistent textual critical methodology that would ever lead you to the exact wording of the Textus Receptus. And here's the example of it. Nowhere else are they going to run off to the Ethiopic. And when the Ethiopic lines up with the Alexandrian as it often does, they'll reject it, because there's no consistency. They're not trying to do textual criticism. They have one goal, and one goal only, "we must defend the TR" and it's not even the TR that they're defending, it's the strain that resulted in the 1633 compilation, well, actually the Hoskier compilation, so it's even just a part of that as it is. They're not defending Erasmus at this point, they're not defending Stephanus at this point, only that element that ends up in what they call the TR.

And so, Beza Vindicated, by an Ethiopic? That he did not even make reference to himself? I gave his own Latin terminology in the book. Passed over in silence. No reason to deal with that. 'Cos that contextualizes things, that's serious history, we're not doing serious history here, we're just throwing stuff out because we're desperate to defend this position, and we will use whatever sources we can get, it doesn't matter if what we used for this verse is completely different for what we used for this verse, which is completely different for what we used for this verse over here, and that we have to have three four five hundred contradictory methodologies, doesn't matter because our ultimate goal is simply the defense of this traditional text. And we will do whatever it takes to do it. Um, there you go, amazing, y'all keep, I really wish you were investing your time doing something that would be useful to the church, and advance the truth. But if you're just gonna keep digging for stuff like this, keep handing it to me and I'll keep explaining to folks, see what I mean? This is why you need to look at what these folks are saying and stay away from it, because wow inconsistency. Sign of that failed argument, big, big, big time. Came out just today..."

After White said these things, I took one month to write the first edition of this book in an article which you are now holding. He refused to read it after many attempts to send draft copies via social media. I challenged him to a debate on the topic which was again replied to with silence. Knowing he would not come to Pakistan any time soon, I noticed that when I was back in Australia some acquaintances of mine were hosting White in a Conference in Brisbane. I was a frequent street preacher and evangelist in Brisbane and the Gold Coast for many years and saw this as an opportunity to hand a printed copy of the study to White personally. So I went up to see Mr White in Brisbane and politely asked him to take the printed form of the text, and he refused it saying that "they would not allow it on the flight!" But only moments before he was holding up a football Jersey that he was taking with him. He announced on his program that he would not read my article.

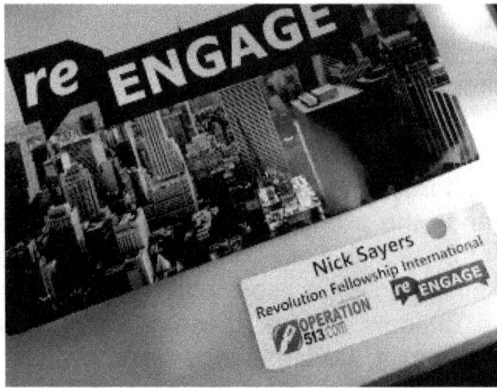

White refused to read the refutation he originally challenged me about when I approached him in Brisbane Australia. He said I was desperate and sad.

Well this book is basically the article White refused to read. I have updated some information on Yahweh, but it is primarily the same article I offered White.

Just recently White did an entire Dividing Line program on this topic, not on the info offered in my article, but upon Tweets on a twitter argument we had on the issue. [171] I suppose seeing he stubbornly refuses to read the information we will never get informed answers on this issue from White, but dribbles of refutation clothed in mockery and slander.

---

[171] https://www.youtube.com/watch?v=yoxQHN_iTJQ

ABOUT THE AUTHOR

Nick Sayers was born in Melbourne Australia, April 13, 1975. He was saved at the age of nineteen. He has since been an avid street preacher having travelled to Papua New Guinea twelve times mostly doing street ministry also many other nations including, Fiji, Indonesia, Philippines, Cambodia, and more recently Pakistan. In 2006 Nick wrote an article in support of the KJV reading of Easter which became popular and was cited by *Answers in Genesis* and *Johnathan Sarfati* of Creation Ministries International. *The conclusions of the article* were supported by *D. A. Waite* and *Jack Moorman*. World leading expert on the English language *David Crystal* also read the article and said that it was good and accurate. Since 2008, he has run the textus-receptus.com website which as of 2019 has had over 44 million page views. The website has thousands of pages of information supporting the Hebrew Masoretic Text and Greek Textus Receptus that underlie the King James Version, and also counteract the false claims against the KJV from modern sceptics, bible agnostics, and cultists.

In 2016 he spent one year in Pakistan working on an Urdu bible translation based upon the Textus Receptus completing the New Testament. The work of the Old Testament is continuing. He has been married since 2015 to a Pakistani Christian whose family are involved in bible translation work based upon the traditional text.

Should the reading of "shalt be" be in the bible at Revelation 16:5? Did Theodore Beza simply make this reading up as James White claims? Is this reading a textual emendation, or is there evidence for the reading? Did the KJV translators and Elzevir's slavishly follow what Beza liked here, rejecting the true reading?

This book examines the claims of that Revelation 16:5 reading is an error in the King James Version and should be changed to read "holy".

I am persuaded that after you have read this book, you will not only be convinced of the reading of "shalt be" (Greek esomenos), but you will see that *all* of the internal and external evidence point to this reading.

James White of Alpha and Omega ministries refused to accept a draft copy of this book and publicly stated he would not read it! What information is he fearful you will know?

5 And I heard the Angel of the waters say, Thou art righteous, O Lord, which art, and wast, and shalt be, because thou hast iudged thus:

King James Version reading of "shalt be" at Revelation 16:5